P9-DED-434

THE BEST PARTY BOOK

1001 Creative Ideas for Fun Parties

THE BEST PARTY BOOK
1001 Creative Ideas for Fun Parties

by
Penny Warner

Illustrated by
Kathy Rogers

𝓶Meadowbrook Press
Distributed by Simon & Schuster
New York

Library of Congress Cataloging-in-Publication Data

Warner, Penny.
    The best party book : 1001 creative ideas for fun parties / by Penny Warner.
        p. cm.
    Previously published as: Penny Warner's party book.
    1. Entertaining. 2. Holidays. I. Title.
GV1471.W27 1192
793.2—dc20   92-8115
                                                      CIP

ISBN 0-88166-188-0
S & S Ordering #: 0-671-78049-2

Editorial Director: Jay Johnson
Editor: Elizabeth H. Weiss
Production Manager: Lynne Cromwell
Production Assistant: Matthew Thurber
Typographer: Jon C. Wright
Cover and Page Design: Tabor Harlow
Cover Art: Tom Lungstrom
Illustrator: Kathy Rogers

© 1992 by Penny Warner

All rights reserved. No part of this book may be reproduced in any form without written
permission from the publisher, except in the case of brief quotations embodied in critical
articles and reviews.

Published by Meadowbrook Press, 5451 Smetana Drive, Minnetonka, MN 55343

BOOK TRADE DISTRIBUTION by Simon & Schuster, a division of Simon and
Schuster, Inc., 1230 Avenue of the Americas, New York, NY 10020.

04 03 02 01   20 19 18 17 16 15 14

Printed in the United States of America

DEDICATION AND THANKS

To Tom, Matt, and Rebecca for being the best family ever.

To Bruce Lansky, Elizabeth Weiss, and Jay Johnson for
being the best book people ever.

CONTENTS

PLANNING THE "BEST PARTY"

Chapter 1

Successful parties are a piece of cake—if you know the secret ingredients: a pinch of sugar, a dash of spice, and a heaping amount of planning! This book will help turn your get-togethers into "Best Parties" if you use the tips and suggestions in the appropriate party chapters with your own good ideas and flair for entertaining. Try these ten easy steps for making your party as fun and inviting as icing on a cake.

1. Choose a theme.

A successful party needs a focus or theme to give it flavor. Once you've chosen the theme you want for your main event, let the creative juices flow and your party will practically host itself.

Almost any party thrives on a theme. A simple shower can become a memorable event if it's designed as a "toy shower" for expectant parents or a "bedroom shower" for the bride- and groom-to-be. Enliven an ordinary birthday party by making it an "over-the-hill" celebration, featuring a black color scheme, mourning armbands, and "denture cleanser" gag gifts. Or throw a "back-to-the-fifties" birthday event with Elvis on the jukebox, yearbook snapshots on the walls, and a prom night motif.

Holiday parties also inspire fun themes. Try a red color scheme for a Valentine's Day party with scarlet food, costumes, and decorations, or a murder-mystery motif for a Halloween bash where the guests dress as detectives and solve a mystery. The possibilities for party themes are limitless.

After you've chosen your theme, it's time to stage the event. If you've decided to host an Academy Awards party and your theme is the glitter and glamour of Hollywood, stage a formal dinner for a small, intimate group, complete with a black tie/evening gown and sunglasses dress code. If you're hosting a Fourth of July picnic, a recipe exchange and an outdoor potluck dinner with red, white, and blue decorations might be just right. An open house, where the guests wander in and out during the afternoon or evening, might be appropriate for a Christmas or Hanukkah gathering.

There are any number of options for your party's theme. You can host a luncheon, brunch, crack-of-dawn breakfast, afternoon tea, late-night supper, or midnight snack party. Or you can try an "anytime" party and feature a wine-tasting, an appetizers-and-dessert buffet, a barbecue or tailgate picnic, a progressive dinner, a potluck, or a come-as-you-are get-together. And don't forget the element of surprise, which adds a touch of drama to parties.

A fun party theme combined with your personal style offers the opportunity to create a unique "Best Party" celebration, so let your creativity and imagination run wild.

2. Create a guest list.

Your party's theme might give you an idea of how many guests to invite. If it doesn't, decide on a comfortable number for your party, and begin the guest list.

Think about the amount of space available for your party in relation to the number of people you're inviting. If you're having a party outdoors, or in a large office, living room, or party room facility, a lengthy guest list is fine. However, if your space is limited, keep the number of guests small to ensure that everyone will be comfortable.

If you're hosting a dinner party with a mixed group of friends, seat each guest next to someone new to help them get acquainted. Or arrange a game to pair off dinner partners, such as "matching famous couples" or "connecting jigsaw puzzle pieces." Seat your guests alternating male and female whenever possible to keep the party more lively and help prevent your guests from forming two separate gender groups. Also, consider your guests' personalities and how well they might mix. For instance, be careful not to seat the "no-nukes" demonstrator next to the nuclear engineer, unless they're the entertainment for the evening. You won't want feuding guests to take the joy out of your special event.

3. Imagine your party in stages.

Hosting a "Best Party" is like directing a play—you begin with a first act, present a lively, action-filled middle, and close with a satisfying ending.

The best way to avoid problems during your party is to picture it in stages—that is, travel through the event in your mind. Party beginnings are usually awkward, but if you remember that the party begins with the first guest, you're sure to produce a success. Take the time to imagine your guests arriving and how you'll welcome them and make each one feel comfortable. Planning the guests' arrival and their introduction to others will help the party get off to a good start.

Next, imagine how and when you'll prepare and serve the food, begin the activities and play games, and allow free time for socializing. Think about how you intend to wrap up the party. Visualize the favors, awards, prizes, and warm good-byes.

If you plan your party's stages in advance, you might foresee problems you can correct ahead of time and avoid unpleasant surprises that could ruin the atmosphere of your party.

4. Plan your menu.

The food at your party doesn't have to be fancy to be good. It's best to keep it simple so you can enjoy the party, too.

Finger foods are easy to make, serve, and eat and are best for large, stand-up parties. You might want to try something different, such as a serve-yourself salad bar, a dessert contest, or a make-your-own-mini-pizza party. Experiment with elaborate and time-consuming dishes only at the most intimate of sit-down dinners. And be sure to try new recipes before the party because they don't always turn out the way you expect!

If you think you'll need some help in the kitchen, consider hiring a high school or college student to assist with preparation, service, and cleanup. Be sure to write down explicit instructions for your amateur servers to minimize problems and maintain pleasant, unobtrusive service. Arrange for the servers to wear special costumes that fit your party's theme. If you prefer to spend most of the time with your guests, you might consider hiring a professional catering service, although they're more expensive and not quite as personal.

If you decide to prepare the food yourself, try to do as much in advance as possible. You'll miss the fun of your own party if you have to spend a lot of time in the kitchen heating up snacks and arranging platters. Simple food can be elegantly prepared, and it's always ready to serve and easy to eat.

Create a menu that relates to your party's theme, if appropriate. Serve Mexican dishes at your Cinco de Mayo festival or an egg cream to welcome the new folks from New York, and keep the champagne flowing at your Academy Awards party.

The question on the mind of most hosts is, "Will there be enough food?" The best recommendation is to make more food than you think you'll need, because you'll probably need it. You can always freeze the leftovers to save yourself from cooking for a few days after the party.

5. Serve food with flair.

Before your party begins, collect enough trays and serving pieces to serve the food. You can borrow them from friends and neighbors or rent the equipment from party goods supply stores and rental outlets. Food looks and tastes better when it's served on elegant or unusual platters and serving pieces.

Make your party a "Best Party" by serving the food in different, but appropriate, ways. You might want to use some of the following items to present your special snacks and treats: wicker baskets, cloth bags, decorative boxes, old-fashioned tins, large copper pots, ceramic mugs, fancy cooking utensils, or large shells.

You can also use food items decoratively. Scoop out fruits and vegetables, such as watermelon, cantaloupe, oranges, pumpkins, or squash, and place the food inside the shells. Or use pita pockets, hollowed French loaves, pizza breads, croissants, tortillas, or cream puff shells to hold the food.

Make sure you have enough tables on which to serve the food. You might want to present food on carts, counters, coffee tables, stools, unusual pieces of furniture, cutting boards, covered TV trays, or bookcases. Or try theme-related items, such as an ironing board or hope chest for a wedding shower or luggage for a bon voyage party.

Cover your tables with decorative tablecloths—or make your own by buying inexpensive lengths of bright, colorful fabric to match your theme. Make your own napkin rings by cutting strips of ribbon and forming them into circles or tying them into bows, or by covering paper towel tubes with fabric or printed paper. You can create original place mats with paper fans, contrasting colors of fabric, maps, large photos, fancy diapers, small straw mats, or inexpensive art reproductions.

"Best Party" Table Ideas

6. Arrange for games and activities.

Fun games can make a party stand out as special among a string of similar get-togethers. The right games and activities will liven up your party and ensure a memorable evening.

Select games and activities best suited to your theme, and make sure they're appropriate for your guests. Try to avoid the standard games that are played at most parties, such as charades or board games. Choosing unique activities will guarantee a "Best Party" success.

If there will be game winners, you'll need to have prizes. Pick out prizes that relate to your theme and can be enjoyed by both men and women, if both sexes are attending your party. Gifts such as a bottle of champagne, a humorous book, tickets to the theater, a coffee mug, a fancy food item, a popular tape, or dinner at a fancy restaurant make good prizes.

Entertainment is a good alternative to games and activities. Hire a musician, comedian, magician, graphologist (handwriting analyst), fortune-teller, disc jockey, juggler, or local celebrity to entertain your guests.

7. Give your party a mood and atmosphere.

Turn your party room into a seaside lagoon, romantic fantasyland, or Mexican festival. All it takes is a little imagination, a few props, and some construction paper to transform an ordinary living room or backyard into another place or time.

Use your party's theme to create an atmosphere that sets the stage, enhances the mood, and lifts the spirits. You might spread a checkered tablecloth for your Italian spaghetti feed, hire a violinist for your romantic Valentine's Day dinner, or hang black balloons and witty epitaphs for your "over-the-hill" party.

Decorations will give your party a sense of flair. Candles or flowers add a nice touch to most party rooms. You can make simple place cards for your table from items such as paper fans, valentines, or baggage claim tickets. Baskets full of appropriate goodies, knick-knacks, and mementos make fun centerpieces. A more imaginative centerpiece will focus everyone's attention on center stage—try a dressed-up baby doll for a baby shower, a few classic record albums for a school reunion, an edible appetizer tree for a Christmas open house, or tagboard cutouts of Academy Award nominees for an Academy Awards party.

The lighting at your party can also affect the mood. Experiment with dimmer switches, candles, colored light bulbs, lanterns, colored paper lamp covers, flashlights, Christmas tree lights, tiki torches, or flashing strobe lights to create the mood you want.

Fill the room with music appropriate to your party's theme. Choose classical for a dinner party, rock and pop for a dance party, country for a Country Music Awards party, or the "Phantom of the Opera" soundtrack for a Halloween bash. Record stores usually carry long-playing tapes and CDs—you might want to purchase some of these so you can be free to enjoy the party rather than constantly attending to the music.

8. Design party invitations.

Create invitations that suit your theme and let your guests know what kind of party they'll be attending. You might want to send your party details on a balloon, paper fan, ticket, postcard, napkin, travel brochure, diaper, baseball card, party hat, wine label, puzzle, magazine ad, or a page from a book—whatever fits your theme. You could put confetti in the envelopes so it sprinkles out when the invitations are opened.

Be sure to read over your guest list a few times to see that you haven't omitted anyone. And don't forget to add an R.S.V.P. request. Include on your invitation the following information:

- Date (and day).
- Time (starting and ending).
- Place (include directions or a map).
- Occasion (birthday, retirement, or shower).
- Party details ("It's a surprise!" or "The shower has a kitchen theme.").
- Attire (black tie, casual, or costumes).

If your party is very formal, send out your invitations three to four weeks before the event. If it's more casual, two weeks in advance is about right.

9. Make a checklist.

Before your "Best Party" lift-off, make a countdown checklist of all the things you need to do. Include on the list any supplies to buy, chores to do, people to call, and other details. There is a sample checklist on p. 9 to help you get started with your party plans. Photocopy the checklist, and use it to help you organize all of the details.

10. Expect to have a good time.

Don't exhaust yourself preparing for the party, or you won't be able to enjoy it. And you've spent too much time and effort to let this happen! So relax—you're party is sure to be a "Best Party" hit!

Spend the day of the party doing the fun things—putting together the final details, indulging in a hot bubble bath or a brisk run through the park, dressing up in a fun outfit, and imagining the good time your guests will have. Now you're ready to greet your guests with a confident smile.

THE "BEST PARTY" CHECKLIST

Three weeks before the party:

☐ Select occasion for party: _____

☐ Select theme and staging: _____

☐ Create guest list.

☐ Send invitations.

    Date of party: _____

    Time (starting, ending): _____

    Place: _____

☐ Plan and select decorations.

☐ Begin collecting materials and creating props.

☐ Prepare menu and grocery list.

☐ Select and hire caterer/serving help (if needed).

A few days before the party:

☐ Call any guests who have not responded.

☐ Buy groceries and beverages.

☐ Prepare and freeze/refrigerate food items that can be made in advance.

☐ Make party costume or select outfit.

One day before the party:

☐ Clean house, party room facility, or office party site.

☐ Set up and arrange party room.

☐ Thaw frozen party foods.

☐ Get out serving pieces.

☐ Coordinate last-minute arrangements with caterer, servers.

The day of the party:

☐ Decorate party room.

☐ Prepare and arrange remaining food.

☐ Coordinate set-up, service, cleanup with hired helpers.

☐ Mentally "travel through" party.

☐ Dress in party outfit.

☐ Await arrival of first guest.

Chapter 2

Before the blushing bride walks down the aisle to meet her groom, she ought to have a wedding shower so she and her husband will have a few household items when the honeymoon is over. In the past, the wedding shower was given only by friends of the bride (not relatives), and it never included the groom. But today anyone can honor the bride with a wedding shower.

Romance is an ideal theme for a wedding shower—after all, that's what love and marriage are all about. There are many ways you can add your own special touches to a wedding shower to create a romantic atmosphere.

First, decide whether you want the shower to be a couples or women-only event. Since many showers today include men, you might ask the bride if she'd like to have her fiancé and his friends attend or if she has any special male friends to invite. Some showers are hosted by the bride's co-workers, so it might be best to invite both the men and women in her office.

There are many options for creating a romantic wedding shower. Consider choosing a specific theme for the party to give it focus and inspire creative gift-buying. Request on the invitations that your guests bring gifts related to the party's theme. If you're hosting a "romance shower," your guests might bring champagne, a collection of love songs on tape, a videotape of *Gone with the Wind,* a box of gourmet chocolates, or tickets to a play.

Here are some other suggestions for theme showers:

- Practical kitchen utensils.
- Sexy bedroom accoutrements.
- Fancy bathroom accessories.
- Elegant dining room gifts for entertaining.
- Romantic honeymoon care packages.
- A food- and entertainment-filled night on the town.

You can also make your shower a "basket surprise" party. Assign a different marriage-related or household theme to each guest, and have each of them fill a basket with appropriate items. For example, if you assign a kitchen basket to a guest, that guest might bring a decorative bread basket lined with a dish towel and filled with small kitchen items, such as a baster, a garlic press, or measuring cups—whatever—as long as they relate to the kitchen and fit in the basket! Here are some other basket suggestions:

- Bath basket (soap, washcloth, bath oil).
- Garden basket (flower seeds, gardening gloves, trowel).
- Bedroom basket (sexy underwear, massage oil, colored condoms).
- Sewing basket (pincushion, needle and thread, patches).
- Romance basket (dinner-for-two coupon, mood music CD, fine-wines cookbook).
- Picnic basket (bottle of champagne, gourmet deli items, book of poetry).
- Entertainment basket (theater or movie tickets, amusement park coupons, X-rated videotape).

Tell your guests to be creative with their baskets. Perhaps they could place the gifts in a wicker basket, flower basket, clothes basket, or even a wastebasket.

Another idea for a theme is a "time of day" shower, which takes a little creativity on the part of the guests. When you invite your guests, assign them a time of day and ask them to bring gifts appropriate for that hour. For example, if you assign 8:00 A.M., your guest might bring an alarm clock, a pair of matching toothbrushes, a cozy bathrobe, some gourmet coffee, or a book of collected newspaper comics. If you assign 2:00 P.M., your guest might bring a bottle of wine, two wine glasses, a romantic tape, and some massage oil for a sexy "afternoon delight." This is a fun and creative party that works well for the bride who has already had a general household shower or owns many household items.

A "Mad-Hatter" shower is another "Best Party" idea where each guest creates an unusual hat covered with shower gifts that are attached by string or wire. Half the fun is seeing friends in their funny hats—the surprise comes when the hats are unraveled and the gifts are revealed to the guest of honor. Naturally, you must award a prize for the best hat—perhaps a special hat of your own creation.

After you've chosen your theme, you'll need to decide what type of shower to have. Luncheon and dessert showers are popular, but any format can work, with a little creativity. You might even hold the shower in a fancy restaurant, and ask your guests to dress to the nines—hats, gloves, sunglasses, and boutonnieres. Then award a prize for the snootiest outfit, such as a toothbrush spray-painted gold or covered with glitter.

See if you can find a friend or relative who's willing to co-host the shower with you. That way, you'll have half the work and twice the ideas.

Invitations

Try a few of these romantic invitation ideas for your wedding shower. You can purchase the materials indicated for these invitations (and others throughout the book) at any craft supply, stationery, or hobby store.

- Photocopy or reprint photographs of the bride and groom,

and cut the pictures into heart shapes. Glue them onto white paper doilies, and outline the heart photos with small pieces of colored cord or piping. Write your party details around the outside of the doily.

- Photocopy the bride and groom's wedding invitation, and use it for the front of your invitation. Fold it over, and write your party details inside.

- Buy imitation wedding rings from a party goods supply store, and tie two of them together with white ribbon. Write your party details on a small white card, and tie the ribbon and rings around it.

- Write your party details on a white heart-shaped card, and place the card in an envelope. Fill the envelope with a tablespoon of colored rice or confetti.

- Buy small bells at a party goods supply store, and tie two of them together with thin ribbon. Then cut a piece of white tagboard into a dove shape, and write your party details on it. Place your "wedding bells" in a small box with the dove-shaped invitation. Mail the invitations in padded envelopes.

Wedding Bells Invitation

- Cut out a heart shape from red construction paper, and write your party details on it. Attach a narrow, white lace border (made from paper or fabric) around the heart.

- Buy a small amount of colored netting, and cut it into 4-inch squares. Cut some plastic wrap into same-sized squares, and place it on the netting. Take a tablespoon of rice, and mix it with a small amount of food coloring and water just until colored. Drain the mixture, and dry it on paper towels. Then drop a tablespoon of the colored rice in the center of your plastic wrap and netting, and tie it into a small package with colored ribbon. Place it in an envelope along with a card containing your party details.

- Draw or photocopy a picture of the bride and groom, and glue it onto tagboard. Cut it into a heart shape, and write your party details on the back. Or cut your design into puzzle pieces, and drop the pieces into an envelope.

- Buy bride-and-groom figurines from a bakery, and attach them to your invitations. Mail them to your guests in padded envelopes or gift boxes.

- Cut out heart shapes from 5-inch squares of red satin. Sew two hearts together, with the outsides facing together. Leave one side of the heart unsewn. Turn the stitched material right side out, and stuff it with sachet or batting. Stitch it closed, and write your party details on the red satin. Mail the invitations in padded envelopes.

- Be sure to include all the party information (date, time, place, guest of honor, kind of shower, and host) and any special details (see p. 9). When selecting colors to use on the invitations, try borrowing from the bride's chosen wedding colors.

Decorations

Keep romance in mind as you decorate for your wedding shower. Here are some suggestions for creating a romantic atmosphere:

- Display lots of helium and standard balloons in your front yard—on trees, gutters, doorknobs, the lamppost, the mailbox—everywhere. Dangle several lengths of white curling ribbon from the end of each balloon. You'll have a stunning display to welcome your guests!

- Fill one wall of your party room with balloons. To do this, tape lengths of string about a foot apart, from ceiling to floor, along one wall. Tie a balloon to each length of string, alternating the bride's colors for a romantic effect.

- Create a "wedding canopy" in your entryway by attaching crepe paper to the center of the ceiling and looping it toward the doorway.

Wedding Canopy

- Set bud vases containing the bride's chosen flowers around the room for a sweet, romantic touch. Or attach single flowers from the bride's chosen bouquet in wide bows, and tie them around the room. If you aren't on a budget, fill your party room with large bouquets and vases of flowers in the bride's chosen colors. You might even rent plants and flowers for a garden-party look.

- Fill clear glass jars, bowls, and decorative vases with colored rice (see p. 15 for rice decorating instructions).

- Collect photographs of the bride and groom from birth to the present, and display them on one wall of your party room.

- Make a "towel cake" in the bride's chosen colors. To do this, fold a washcloth, hand towel, and bath towel (new, of course, to be given as a gift at the end of the party) lengthwise into thirds, rolling them up, and securing the ends with small safety pins. Set the rolled bath-towel layer on a large doily, the hand-towel layer in the center of the bath towel, and the washcloth layer on top of the hand towel. Loop velveteen ribbon around the layers to make "icing," and secure with pins. Top the whole thing off with a fresh corsage or bride-and-groom figurines from a bakery.

Towel Cake

- Have a blowup made from a photograph of the bride and groom, and hang it on the wall. Give it to the guest of honor as a gift after the party.
- Have blowups made from the bride and groom's baby pictures, and hang them together on the wall. Give them to the guest of honor as a gift after the party.
- Rent *Casablanca*, and have it playing on your TV set (without the sound).
- Hang posters of famous romantic couples, such as "Bogey" and Bacall, Scarlett and Rhett, Lucy and Ricky, and Mickey and Minnie.
- Hang a wreath on the door with something old (an antique knickknack), something new (a fun pair of earrings), something borrowed (a library book about marriage), and something blue (a blue nightie).
- Make corsages out of small household items, such as a new kitchen sponge, wire whisk, or potato peeler, tied with ribbons and flowers. Have your guests wear them during the party, and give them to the guest of honor when the party is over. Or make one large corsage for the bride to wear.
- Cut out red paper hearts from construction paper, and hang them from the ceiling with white yarn. Or cut out white paper doves, and hang them from the ceiling.
- Play romantic love songs on your tape or CD player.
- Have white candles burning throughout the room.

Games and Activities

Games are popular, traditional shower activities. In keeping with the romance theme, here are a few game ideas for the young at heart:

The Wedding Night

While the bride opens her shower gifts, discreetly write down her oohs and ahs, exclamations, and shrieks of joy. As you take notes, write down only the comments that could be interpreted as a reaction to the "wedding night." After she has opened all her gifts, make the following announcement:

> There's an ancient marriage prophesy that states that whatever the bride says during the gift-opening ceremony at her wedding shower will be the very same words she will say during her wedding night. If any of you happen to be passing by the newly-weds' bedroom door on that sacred night, here are a few of the things you might hear.

Then read back all of the comments you wrote down as the guest of honor opened her gifts. You should get some wonderfully embarrassing statements that sound hilarious when read out-of-context, such as: "Ooh, it's just what I've always wanted!" "I've never had one of these before!" or "Wow—it's enormous!"

The Newlywed Game

This game will take a little preparation—but it's well worth it! If the party is for women only, call the groom and ask him some questions about himself, such as: "What's your favorite dessert?" "Where did you go on your first date with your fiancée?" "What's your worst habit?" "What time do you go to bed?" "What meal does your fiancée cook the best?" "What was your last fight about?" "What makes you jealous?" and "What do you sleep in?" Ask him not to tell his fiancée about the phone call or the game.

Write each question on the front side of a 5-by-8-inch card and each answer on the back (or better yet, have the groom make a special appearance for this game to answer the questions himself). Pass out one question card to each guest, and have them take turns reading the questions aloud *without* letting the bride answer. Have each guest estimate how many right answers the bride will get—remember, she has not been told about the game ahead of time. (Be sure there are plenty of questions to go around at least once; perhaps twice). When everyone has guessed how many answers the bride will get right, have them read their questions again, and then have the bride try to answer them. Count up the number of correct answers given by the bride, and award a prize to the guest who came closest to the actual number.

This game works well with couples, too. Just follow the format of the television show "The Newlywed Game" if you plan to invite men and women to your wedding shower.

Married Names

Pass out paper and pencil, and ask your guests to write down the names of famous people who, if married, would form an interesting married name. For example, "If Phyllis Diller married Dobie Gillis, she'd be Phyllis Gillis." Or, "If Joan Collins married Tom Mix, she'd be Joan Collins-Mix." Or, "If Virginia Woolf married Thomas Mann, she'd be Virginia Woolf-Mann." Award a prize to the guest who comes up with the funniest name combination.

Rice Race

Fill several balloons with colored rice (see p. 15 for rice decorating instructions), blow the balloons up very full, and tie them off. Divide your guests into two teams, and line them up in facing rows. Give your guests two forks each. Have them, on the count of three, pass a balloon to the first person on both teams: Each must take the balloons with forks only and pass them to the next in line. Be careful—too much pressure or sharp tines can easily pop the balloons! The balloons are passed down the lines in the same forks-only manner. The team with the balloon that makes it all the way down the line first, wins. If a balloon is popped along the way, a new balloon is begun again at the start. As the guest of honor leaves the party, have her stop outside, and pop the rest of the rice-filled balloons over her head.

Pin the G-string on the "Hunk"

This game is for women only and also works well for a bachelorette party. Buy a large poster of your favorite male exotic dancer or a good-looking celebrity. Make a paper G-string for each guest, plus one extra. Glue the extra one over the "G-string" area of the "hunk," and hang the poster on the wall at eye-level. At game time, stick a thumbtack into each of the G-strings (or back each with a loop of tape), blindfold your guests, and one at a time have them try to pin or tape their G-strings to the appropriate place on the pinup. Give the poster to the guest who comes closest to the G-string area.

Beauty Ads

Before the party, cut out some beauty ads from magazines like *Glamour, Vogue,* or *Self,* omitting the product names. Mount the ads onto construction paper or tagboard. To play, hold up the ads or pass them around, and have your guests try to guess the names of the products and write their answers on a piece of paper. Give the guest who gets the most correct answers a beauty product to take home.

Give-a-Hint

On your party invitations, ask each guest to bring a "helpful hint" that goes along with his or her gift. It can be a household hint or a marital hint—funny or serious—as long as it relates to the shower gift. As each gift is opened, ask the guest who brought it to read his or her helpful hint. Be sure they leave the hints with the gifts after all of them have been opened.

True Confessions

This game is fun for both a couples or women-only party. Have each guest take a turn answering the question, "How did you meet your husband/wife (or boyfriend/girlfriend)?" If you want, you can go a step further and ask, "What was the most embarrassing moment during your relationship?" If you've invited an especially close-knit group, try a round of telling some *"first time* with your partner" stories. Award prizes for the most interesting accounts.

How to Have a Perfect Marriage

Divide sheets of paper in half by drawing a line in the center; the number of papers should equal the number of guests. Write down a typical marital problem on the top half of each sheet, such as "If your husband wants to watch football all weekend . . ." "If your wife flirts with another man . . ." "If you burn the toast . . ." or "If your mother-in-law drives you crazy . . ." Be as creative as you want, but continue to use the "If . . ." format.

Pass out the papers to each of your guests, and ask everyone to write a piece of advice for the problem on the *bottom* half, completing the sentence. For example, if a guest reads, "If you burn the toast . . ." he or she might answer with ". . . get another piece."

After everyone has written down an answer, tear off the top half of the paper and mix up the problems; then mix up the answers, and pass them out to your guests. Ask the guest of honor to pick a problem and read it aloud, and have the first person to her left read the answer, followed by the next person for the next question, and so on. You should get some funny pieces of scrambled advice like, "If you burn the toast, unplug the TV set."

Here Comes the Bride

If you have a small group, use the bride for this game. If you have a large group, divide your guests up into teams and choose a "bride" for each team. Hand each group several rolls of toilet paper, and have them "dress" the bride. If you have teams, award prizes for creativity, beauty, silliness, and so on.

Refreshments

In keeping with the romantic theme and atmosphere of your shower, here are some "love-ly" treats to try:

Drinks

- Start your guests off with a glass of champagne garnished with a strawberry or maraschino cherry.
- Serve slushy strawberry daiquiris. Mix ½ pint strawberry ice cream and 2 ounces rum in the blender, and whirl until smooth. Quick and delicious!

Appetizers

- Baked Brie topped with sliced strawberries and green apple slices makes a beautiful and delicious appetizer.
- For a hearty treat, bake Brie inside a hollowed-out, round loaf of French bread for 10 minutes at 350°.
- Melon balls wrapped in prosciutto and secured with fancy toothpicks look inviting in a scooped-out cantaloupe shell. Or fill an ornately carved watermelon shell with a variety of fresh fruits.

Luncheon foods

- Make mini-croissant sandwiches filled with deviled ham or turkey salad.

- Prepare a few varieties of quiche. Beat 3 eggs, and then add 1¼ cups light cream, ½ teaspoon salt, ¼ teaspoon pepper, ½ teaspoon dry mustard, and ¼ teaspoon nutmeg for each quiche. Then pour the mixture over a partially pre-baked shell filled with your favorite "filler" combination. Try: broccoli and ham, sautéed onion and bacon, mushroom and green pepper, crab and avocado, or shrimp and chicken. Bake at 375° for 40 minutes until the center is set. Let it stand 10 minutes, cut it into wedges or small squares, and serve. Serves eight.

Desserts

- Serve ladyfingers topped with your favorite frosting and trimmed with walnuts—they're simple and elegant.

- Dip strawberries in semisweet and white chocolate, and arrange them on a large platter.

- A dessert as simple as French vanilla ice cream in champagne or sherbet glasses and topped with white sugar doves (available at confectionary or bakery supply stores) is an elegant addition to any party.

Cakes

- Decorate your cake (or have it done at a bakery) with sugar doves, imitation gold rings, or flowers in the bride's chosen colors. You might want to have a small version of a wedding cake, or have it made in the shape of a book, to resemble a wedding album.

- If you're serving cake for dessert, you might want to add some sherbet on the side, in flavors that match the bride's chosen colors.

Prizes, Gifts, and Favors

You'll need some romantic prizes for the game winners and some fun favors for the rest of your guests.

Prizes

- Coffee mugs covered with hearts and a mushy message.
- Box of candy.
- Bottle of champagne.
- Romance novel.
- Tape or CD by Michael Bolton, Julio Iglesias, or other romantic singer.
- Dinner for two at a romantic restaurant.
- Romantic movie on videotape, such as *Ghost, Love Story*, or *Casablanca*.
- Picnic basket for two.
- His and her matching socks.
- Board games like "Scruples" or "The Dating Game."
- Weekend reservations at a Bed & Breakfast or country inn.

Gifts

- Box of stationery with the bride's new married name embossed at the top.
- Return-address labels with the bride's new married name.
- Brass nameplate for the front door inscribed with the couple's married names.
- Photo album for all the wedding or shower pictures.
- Books about love, marriage, or sex.
- Plants for the new home.
- Sexy nightie.
- Pair of white silk stockings or panties for the wedding.
- The wedding invitation in an elegant frame.
- Baby picture of the bride's fiancé.

- Enlarged photograph of the couple.

Favors

- Colorful Jordan almonds wrapped in netting and tied with white ribbon.
- Romance magazines, rolled up and tied with ribbon.
- Small heart-shaped boxes filled with Red Hots.
- Silk roses or flowers from the arrangements used for the party.
- Fancy panties.
- Love coupons to give to a spouse or partner.
- Small book of poems.

BACHELOR AND BACHELORETTE PARTIES

Chapter 3

Bachelor and bachelorette parties are a fun tradition for many soon-to-be-married couples. While the bachelor party (or "stag") is usually less formal, the bachelorette party (or "doe") gives women an opportunity to get a bit wicked. Many women use the opportunity to visit a male strip joint or to hire male strippers or dancers to drop in during the party. The surprise "guests" usually arrive in some kind of costume like a police uniform or cowboy get-up, switch on a cassette player, and start dancing as they peel off their clothes down to a G-string or bikini briefs. You can find exotic male dancers in the Yellow Pages under "Entertainers." Keep in mind that some women may feel offended by this kind of show—if you suspect a guest might not enjoy this, phone her ahead of time to prepare her.

You can also make your bachelorette party a lingerie party—ask your guests to wear sexy nightwear, and have a lingerie hostess (from any lingerie store or party sales group) come to the party to show the latest styles. You might want to invite men to this party, too. It's fun if they dress in black tie!

As for how to throw a bachelor party—it couldn't be easier. Just provide good food and entertainment, and everyone will have fun. If you're stumped for ideas, read on . . . .

Invitations

Here are a few invitation "teasers" for your bachelor or bachelorette party. Include the date, time, place, guest of honor, special instructions or theme, and host.

Bachelorette Party

- Buy paper underwear at a lingerie store, and write your party details on the back.

- Buy sexy postcards or tear out a few pictures of handsome men from magazines, and write your party information in the open spaces.

- Buy some inexpensive garters, and tie a card with your party details to them.

Garter Invitation

- Tear out a page from a *Frederick's of Hollywood* or *Victoria's Secret* catalog, and write your party details on it.

- Put an inviting "hunk" on the front of your invitation. Many stationery or gift stores sell cards with pictures of pinup men on them—perfect as a background for your party details.

Bachelor Party

- Invitations have not been traditionally sent out for stag parties. You can, however, substitute female pinups for the male ones in the bachelorette party invitation ideas. Tear out a page from *Playboy, Penthouse,* etc., and write your party details on it.

- Buy some cheap cigars, and tie a card with your party details to them.

- Or just phone the guys, and tell them to show up!

Decorations

With a raunchy, racy party in mind, decorate accordingly to put your guests in the proper mood.

Bachelorette Party

- Buy *Playgirl* or another risqué magazine, and tape the centerfold to the walls.

- Buy some posters of popular male celebrities—preferably with their shirts off—and tape them to the walls. You can use these posters as prizes for the game winners, too.

- Make a basket of items for the honeymoon night—cologne, breath mints, body paint, sexy panties, and a sex manual—and tie it with a white ribbon to use as a centerpiece. Give the basket to the bride as a gift.

- Buy matching pairs of postcards of several different male pinups, and place one at each place setting. Put the other half of each set in a sewn-up pair of jockey shorts (or a bag), and let each guest pull out a card. Then have everyone match their cards to the pinups on the table to determine their place settings.

Bachelor Party

- Posters of sexy women or pages from risqué magazines make appropriate wall decorations.

- Cigars, beer cans, condoms, sex toys—anything raunchy and "male"—can be used for centerpieces, table decorations, or party favors.
- Or skip the decorations and just switch on the TV and VCR!

Games and Activities

To make your party exciting, plan a few surprises in the way of entertainment and activities. Here are a few ideas to keep the party rolling:

Bachelorette Party

- If you hire a male stripper, plan for him to arrive toward the end of the party to ensure that all the guests will be there. You'll definitely want to keep his visit a secret from the bride, but you might also want to keep your other guests in the dark so he surprises everyone!
- Place items that are primarily associated with men in sealed, doubled lunch bags. You might include items such as a can of shaving cream, a pair of jockey shorts, a bottle of men's cologne, a little black book, and a condom. Have each of your guests feel the outside of the sealed bags, and write down what they think the items are. The guest with the most correct answers wins. For a prize, you might give away the items in the bag.
- Buy a large poster of the bride's favorite male celebrity. A full-body shot works best. With paper and pencil, trace your favorite body part, outline it in black felt-tip pen, and photocopy it for your guests. At game time, play "Pin the (Body Part) on the Hunk."
- Pick out some words from the dictionary that sound a little risqué, but aren't. Then pass out paper and pencil for a refresher course in "Sex Education." Read your pre-chosen words, and have your guests make up definitions aloud. Award a point to any guest who gets the definition correct— but most answers will probably be incorrect, and funny. Try these words if you're stuck: fug (bad smell), dastard

(coward), dik-dik (African antelope), sextant (measuring instrument), titivate (to dress up). The guest with the most points or the funniest answer wins.

Bachelor Party

- If you hire a female stripper, follow the rules of thumb indicated for the bachelorette party.
- Belly dancers might be a welcome alternative to strippers, and you could decorate with an exotic theme out of the *Arabian Nights.* Suspend a parachute from your party room ceiling to create a billowy tent effect—and bring out the dancing girls.
- Television-viewing might be your best bet for entertainment. An X-rated movie and a lot of good-natured digs at the groom ("Look what you're giving up!") are bachelor party traditions.

Refreshments

Most bachelorette parties are held in the evening, with just drinks, snacks, and dessert. You may want to look at the Wedding Shower chapter for more ideas (see p. 22). For a bachelor party, make sure there's plenty of food!

Bachelorette Party

- Fill cream puffs with pistachio ice cream, and top them with caramel sauce.
- Layer parfait glasses with mint chocolate-chip ice cream and graham cracker crumbs. Top with whipped cream and a sprinkle of mini chocolate chips.
- Make a berry whip by blending 1 cup frozen (in syrup) or fresh strawberries, 1 cup plain yogurt (lowfat or whole), 1 tablespoon lemon juice, and 2 teaspoons honey in the blender. Blend only until all the ingredients combine into a thick, creamy mixture.
- Tell your guests all your refreshments are aphrodisiacs.

Bachelor Party

- Make sure there's plenty of beer, soft drinks, pretzels, and other deluxe munchies on hand.

- Set up a make-your-own submarine sandwich table—include breads, spreads, vegetable slices, lettuce, cold cuts, and cheeses.

- Give your guests a sugar rush with a do-it-yourself ice cream sundae table—include several ice cream flavors, sliced fruit, nuts, sprinkles, and a sinful collection of toppings.

Prizes, Gifts, and Favors

An evening of slightly unbridled revelry requires slightly unbridled prizes and party favors, too.

Bachelorette Party

- For prizes, give game winners a sexy book or magazine, or some sexy underwear.

- If your guests need gift ideas, suggest sexy lingerie or underwear, perfume, or a sex manual.

- If you want to give your guests favors, try lingerie catalogs, sexy underwear, or romance novels.

- A fun bridal gift is a honeymoon kit containing phony birth control pills, a back scrub brush, bubble bath, champagne, a sex manual, a romance novel, bonbons, aspirin, and any other fun items for that special night.

Bachelor Party

- Embarrass your guest of honor with gifts like a sex toy, a sex manual, revealing underwear, a nightshirt, condoms, pornography, or a honeymoon kit filled with male-oriented accessories.

- Keep the prizes and favors simple—try a case of beer or some after-shave.

- Take Polaroid photos of your guests with the stripper or belly dancer. Give them to your guests as party favors.

- If the activities include heavy indulging, serve black coffee to your guests, arrange taxi rides home, and pass out Alka Seltzer for the "morning after."

Chapter 4

The birth of a baby is an exciting time for new parents, and a baby shower is a celebration of that joy and enthusiasm. When hosting a shower, the first decision you'll need to make is when to have it—before or after the baby is born.

Some parents-to-be prefer to have a baby shower after the baby is born because that way they'll receive gifts appropriate to the baby's sex. (And some pregnant women are uncomfortable in the last few weeks of pregnancy and may not feel up to attending the event.) Others prefer a more traditional shower before the baby comes. Unless the shower is intended as a surprise—which may bring on labor if it's too big a surprise!—it's a good idea to ask the prospective parents when they want the baby shower to be held.

Next you'll want to decide whether the shower will be a women-only event or include men. Some showers are office parties, in which case you should try to include your guest of honor's male co-workers. More and more men are becoming involved with every aspect of parenthood, including the baby shower, so be sure to ask the father if he'd like to join the party, too.

There are many fun shower themes to choose from. You can offer the new parents a shower with a baby gift theme so they can stock their nursery. Try some of the following:

- Baby clothes (diapers, rompers, sleepers).
- Baby toys (rattles, music boxes, stuffed animals).
- Bath items (plastic tub, washcloths, bath towels).

You can hold a "time of day" shower and ask that gifts be related to the appointed hour (see p. 13 for more details). For example, if the assigned time is noon, your guest might bring mealtime items such as dishes, bottles, or bibs. Or if the assigned time is 7:00 P.M., your guest might bring bedtime items such as sleepers, bedding, or musical stuffed animals.

You might have a shower theme devoted to outfitting the nursery instead of the baby, with guests bringing items such as posters, mobiles, furniture, bedding, and layette supplies.

You might even throw a shower where the emphasis is on the new parents instead of the baby and request that guests bring gifts for the expectant parents. Here are some fun suggestions:

- Have guests bring a special gift for Mom. This would be a good time to fill her maternity suitcase with a new nightie, baby-care books, travel-size bottles of shampoo and body lotion, or a breast-feeding blouse.
- If Dad is invited, you could ask each guest to bring along a gift especially for him, such as *TV Guide* for those late-night feedings, a copy of *David, We're Pregnant!* or *Hi, Mom! Hi, Dad!* by Lynn Johnston (Meadowbrook Press, 1992), a copy of *How to Be a Pregnant Father* by Peter Mayle (Lyle Stuart, 1977), a copy of *Babies and Other Hazards of Sex* by Dave Barry (Rodale Press, 1984), or a rubber lap protector.

You might decide to give your party a general theme, such as "storks," "teddy bears," "sugar and spice," or "coming soon from the cabbage patch," with invitations, decorations, and refreshments that go along with the theme. And once you choose a theme, you can decide whether to have a brunch, luncheon, dessert, or afternoon tea. Just be sure to check with the new parents first so they'll be at their best for this special occasion.

Invitations

There are lots of creative ways to invite guests to your baby shower, so begin your party plans with an invitation related to your theme. Include a request for each guest to bring along one of his or her own baby pictures for a game. Here are some suggestions for your baby shower invitations:

- You can create little diaper invitations by cutting out triangles from pink and blue construction paper or felt. Write your party details on one side of the triangle with a felt-tip pen, and then fold the triangle like a diaper and secure it with a cute diaper pin from an infant and maternity gift shop.

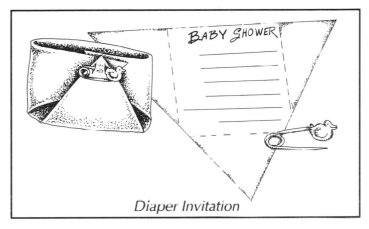

Diaper Invitation

- Cut out pictures of babies from magazines, and glue them onto a piece of tagboard with a cartoon bubble containing your party details above the babies' heads.
- Send your guests a bubble gum cigar with a tag announcing, "It's a baby shower!" Write your party details on the tag.
- Borrow baby pictures of the expectant parents, and photocopy them. Arrange the photos together on a pink or blue tagboard card, and write your party details on the reverse side.
- Fold a sheet of green construction paper in half, and draw a picture of a cabbage. Cut out the cabbage with the fold at the bottom so you can open up the cabbage. Glue a baby picture inside, and put your party information beside it.

- Pick up some miniature plastic baby dolls or other baby decorations at a party goods supply store, and tie them with pink and blue ribbon to a card containing your party details.
- Cut out pink or blue pacifiers from tagboard, and write your party details on one side. Tie with ribbon.
- Check a variety store for baby paper dolls. Cut out the dolls and clothing, and write your party details on one of the outfits.
- Make tiny birth certificates using quality paper and careful handwriting. Fill in your party details instead of baby details.
- Cut out or create pictures of teddy bears or storks to use as invitations.
- Cut out small handprints or footprints, and write your party details on one side.
- Create your own rhyme, borrowing from an old nursery rhyme or other favorite, and change the words to fit your party. For example, "Roses are red, violets are blue, we're having a shower, and hope you'll come, too." Decorate your invitation with cutouts from an inexpensive nursery rhyme book.
- Make a hospital bracelet like the one attached to babies after birth. To do this, cut white tagboard into strips, and write your party information on both sides. Cover the strips with clear Contact paper, and form a circle by punching a small hole on both ends and tying them together.
- Tear out a page from an old baby name book, and write your party information around the edges.
- Send a picture of the very pregnant mom-to-be glued to a card with all your party information on the back.
- Cut out three squares from pink, blue, and yellow construction paper. Draw the letters A, B, and C on them so they look like blocks, overlap them and tape or glue them together, and write your party information on the back of each one.

Decorations
• • • • • • • • • • • • • • • •

With a little imagination and a few props, you can turn your party room into a make-believe nursery. Try some of the following suggestions to set the mood for your baby shower:

- Cover the table with a pink or blue paper tablecloth, and set plates of the opposite color around it. Or cover the table with a baby blanket, and put a plastic cover on top to protect it.

- Make name tags for your guests from pink and blue triangles cut from felt and folded into diapers. Make place mats from cloth diapers dyed pink and blue. Or make pink and blue construction paper place mats, and glue on pictures of babies cut out from magazines.

- Write your guests' names on the outside of small felt diapers, and pin them to guests as they arrive.

- Before the shower, ask each guest to bring an old baby picture. Collect and mount the photos on a sheet of yellow construction paper as your guests come in the door (use masking tape on the back of the photos). Be sure to write each guest's name on the construction paper before you mount the photo so you know who's who. Carefully tape the construction paper "frame" to one wall in the party room (making sure that no names show) to use for a game later on.

- If you can find a "Super Baby" pajama outfit or "Super Hero" underwear (available at many department and discount stores in the infant/toddler section), dress up a baby doll or Cabbage Patch Kid in the outfit and set it in an infant seat (or other piece of baby equipment) in the center of the table or party room.

- Hang cute diaper pins from the ceiling using pink, yellow, and blue ribbon. Or hang miscellaneous baby items, such as rattles, blocks, or pacifiers instead. Cut out small storks from plain white paper, and hang them from the ceiling.

- Place baskets full of baby items in the center of the table to use as a centerpiece. Or make a centerpiece from a collection of baby toys, such as a stack of small, colorful blocks.

- Borrow some dolls and doll furniture, and set up a little

display for a centerpiece.

- Tie pink and blue balloons to the back of each chair.
- Place cabbages cut out from green construction paper around the walls, with pictures of babies peeping over the cabbage leaves.
- Double up a pair of pastel baby socks, and pin them together as a corsage for the guest of honor.
- Serve party drinks in clear plastic baby bottles (or glass ones, if you have them). Decorate them with pink and blue ribbon, and use pink and blue straws.
- Cut out tiny baby clothes from pink, blue, and yellow felt (or use real baby outfits), and pin them to a small clothesline. Hang the clothesline on the wall, or secure it to stands, and use it as a centerpiece for your table.

Clothesline Centerpiece

- Buy inexpensive bibs, or make them from terrycloth or plastic fabric, and use them as place mats.
- Play nursery music in the background during your shower.

Games and Activities

You and your guests will think of those tiny bundles of joy when

40

you play these baby shower games:

Baby Food Taste Test

This is a terrific game that will put a lot of funny expressions on your guests' faces! Buy eight jars of baby food (get a variety—cereal, fruit, vegetables, meat, and mixtures) and remove or cover the labels with heavy paper so they can't be read. Write a number on the side of each jar with a felt-tip pen, and keep track of the flavors by number on a separate sheet of paper. Pass out paper plates, plastic spoons, and paper and pencils to all players. Ask your guests to make eight circles on their plates and label each with a number, *outside* the circle. Then place a plastic spoon in each of the baby food jars.

Begin the game by announcing that since the guest of honor's baby will have to eat this stuff, it's only fair that all the baby shower guests taste it first. (Wait till you see the reaction to this!) Pass around the first jar, and ask everyone to spoon out a small amount of baby food onto the first circle on their plate, and taste it with their spoon. Have your guests write what flavor they think they're tasting on their sheet of paper, keeping their answer to themselves—no cheating! When all eight jars have been passed around and guesses written down, announce the real flavors, and have everyone count their correct answers. It's rare that anyone guesses them all.

Baby Business

Tear out eight to ten pictures of baby products from magazines like *American Baby, Parents,* or *Working Mother,* and cut off the names of the products. For example, you might find a photo of a teething baby who's crying and cut off the word "Numzit." Glue the magazine photos onto pink and blue construction paper or tagboard. Ask your guests to write down the product name as you hold up each card for all to see. The guest with the most correct answers is the winner.

Guess Who?

Now it's time to use all those old baby pictures you told everyone to bring! Have your guests look closely at the photos and guess who's who. The guest with the most correct answers is the winner.

Guess the Baby Item

Collect ten baby items such as a nose syringe, thermometer, medicine dropper, rattle, pacifier, comb, diaper, baby book, rubber pants, and bottle brush. Buy twenty paper bags, preferably ten in pink and ten in blue.

"Guess the Baby Item"

Place one bag inside another for double-bag durability, and put one of the ten baby items in each bag. Number the bags from one to ten on the outside, and staple each bag closed. Tell your guests to feel the *outside* of the bags and try to guess what baby item is inside. Pass each bag around, let everyone feel it for about thirty seconds, and then pass it to the left. When all the guests have had a chance to handle the bags and write their answers, open them up and pull out the baby items. Present the baby items to the guest of honor and a prize to the winner.

Belly Button Estimate

Give all your guests a 5-foot length of yarn, and ask them to mark off with a knot the circumference of the expectant mother's tummy. Then measure the pieces around her waist to see who's closest to the actual measurement. Or ask your guests how many diaper pins it would take to go around the guest of honor's belly. Then connect enough pins to fit around Mom, and determine the winner. Give the diaper pins to the guest of honor as a gift and a prize to the winner.

Take My Advice

As the expectant mother opens each shower gift, ask the guests to give her one piece of advice that might be helpful in the first few months of parenthood. (You might want to share some of the worst advice as well.)

Another version of this activity is to pass around a nicely-bound blank book, and have each guest write a few "gems of motherly wisdom" on raising children. After the guests have had a chance to write down their comments, let the guest of honor read all the entries aloud.

Good Reading

Ask each guest to bring a poem, an excerpt from a story, or some other printed passage that expresses an aspect of parenthood. Have each guest read his or her selection to the guest of honor as she opens each shower gift.

Crib Notes

On small slips of paper, write down an old-wives' tale, a line of poetry, a quote from a baby book, or some other passage about childrearing. Place the slips of paper in a basket, and then ask each guest to pick a slip from the basket, read the quote aloud, and make a comment about it. Don't let your guests read the quotes ahead of time—this should be spontaneous.

Child Development

Write down some typical childhood events on slips of paper. You might include such milestones as baby's first tooth, first step, first word, or first haircut; or junior's first day of kindergarten, first trip to the dentist, first bike, or first day at camp.

Number each slip in order of development, and give one to each guest. Call the events by number, and have the guest with that number act out a parent's reaction to baby's newest development. Have the rest of the party members guess the stage.

Refreshments
● ● ● ● ● ● ● ● ● ● ● ● ● ● ● ● ● ● ● ●

Since your guest of honor is eating for two, you'll need plenty of food! Check the Wedding Shower chapter (see p. 22) for refreshment ideas, or try one of the following:

Drinks

- Pregnant women should not drink alcohol, so serve a nonalcoholic punch made from a clear, decaffeinated soft drink and cranberry juice, or club soda and fruit juice.

- Float large spoonfuls of raspberry sherbet in your punch bowl, and add a spoonful to each glass as you serve the punch.

Appetizers

- Make a fruit pizza by rolling out sugar cookie dough and baking it according to package directions, until lightly browned. Top the baked crust with fruit slices, such as strawberries, mandarin oranges, kiwi, and blueberries. Pour over an instant lemon meringue filling to set, and refrigerate until serving time.

- Keep Arrowroot cookies or other teething biscuits in a candy jar for guests to nibble on before lunch is served.

Luncheon Foods

- Have a bakery tint a few loaves of bread pink and blue for your sandwiches. Fill the sandwiches with salmon and cream cheese, or cream cheese (tinted, if you wish) mixed with walnuts and raisins.

- Prepare a healthful and tasty Chinese chicken salad for a nice balance to sweets. Shred a head of lettuce or Nappa cabbage into a bowl, and add 2 cups each pea pods, bean sprouts, and sliced green and red bell pepper. Then sauté 4 half chicken breasts (cut in strips) in 2 tablespoons oil combined with $\frac{1}{2}$

cup soy sauce and 3 tablespoons brown sugar. (Sauté briefly, turning frequently.)

In another pan, sauté 2 packages ramen noodles (precooked—do *not* add soup mix), $^3/_4$ cup sesame seeds, and $^1/_2$ cup slivered almonds in $^1/_4$ cup butter until golden brown. Combine mixture with chicken and toss into lettuce (or cabbage) and vegetables with the following dressing: $^1/_2$ cup oil, $^1/_4$ cup red wine vinegar, 2 tablespoons soy sauce, and $^1/_4$ cup sugar. Serves six to eight.

Desserts

- Offer petit fours, ladyfingers, or puff pastries for a delicate and tasty dessert.
- Serve your guests elegant sherbets in cleaned-out baby food jars with little silver spoons. For fun, pass around a jar of pickles to go with the sherbet!
- Serve hollowed-out oranges filled with orange sherbet and topped with whipped cream, or make meringue shells and fill with strawberries and blueberries. Top with a dollop of whipped cream, tinted pink or blue.

Cakes

- A teddy bear cake or a decorated cake with pink or blue booties (or storks, cabbages, or whatever fits your theme) makes a nice centerpiece and feeds a hungry crowd.
- Ask a bakery to make a cake in the shape of a rattle, diaper, or baby bottle and decorate appropriately.

Prizes, Gifts, and Favors

Prizes

- Copy of Dave Barry's *Babies and Other Hazards of Sex* (Rodale Press, 1984) or *Separated at Birth?* (Doubleday, 1988).
- Gag gifts, such as packages of contraceptives or a home pregnancy test.

- Any romantic item that can be shared with a partner—a block of cheese, a loaf of French bread, or a bottle of wine.
- Items that contain the word "baby," such as a Baby Ruth candy bar, Sugar Babies, Babe cologne, or a book about Babe Ruth.
- Book about where babies come from.
- Clear baby bottle full of mints, nuts, or jelly beans.

Gifts

- Ask all your guests to contribute to one large gift, such as a baby swing, and to also bring along one small gift.
- List of all the parks, baby classes, pediatricians, and discount baby clothing stores in the community.
- Have each guest bring a male and female name suggestion on a cute card, along with a little history about the name and a list of famous people with the same name—recommend Bruce Lansky's *The Baby Name Personality Survey* (Meadowbrook Press, 1990) for baby names and information. Ask the expectant mother which name is her favorite, and award a prize to the guest who suggested it.
- Ask each guest to bring a box of disposable diapers wrapped in fancy paper and ribbons, along with a gift. Or ask your guests to wrap their diaper boxes in plain pink, blue, or yellow paper. Then cut out large alphabet letters from construction paper, glue them to the sides of the boxes, and set them up in your party room to look like a gigantic stack of baby blocks. You might ask your guests to do the decorating, baby-block style.
- Baby-care, baby-naming, or baby-keepsake books.
- Coupons worth several hours of baby-sitting, housecleaning, or laundry help.
- Ask each guest to sign up for one night of bringing dinner to the new family.
- Have each guest create a quilt square in a particular theme (the alphabet, toys, colors, and so on) and ask someone to sew them all together before the party. Then present the quilt to the

guest of honor as a wonderful finale.

- Coupon for a portrait of the new baby and a silver frame. Or have each guest bring along a roll of film nicely wrapped so the new parents can take lots of pictures of their newborn. (Make certain the film is right for the guest of honor's camera!)
- Start a savings account or go in on a savings bond for the new baby.
- Tiny T-shirt with the words "Class of 2001" (or whatever year the baby will graduate from high school).

Favors

- Teddy bear pin or other youthful accessory.
- Small gift for your guests' own children, such as a coloring book, crayons, a Golden Book, or small puzzle. (Even if some don't have children, perhaps the favor could be given to a niece, nephew, or neighbor's child.)
- Favors that are easy to make and fun, such as a fake bottle of birth control pills. To do this, find some old medicine bottles (or buy them from a pharmacy) and fill them up with small, round candies. Make labels that read, "Birth Control Pills: To prevent pregnancy, take one daily," or some other silly instructions.
- Box of Sugar Babies or a Baby Ruth candy bar.

Chapter 5

Birthday parties are a joy to give, especially when they're in honor of a special friend or relative. Your party can be a great boost for someone who dreads those milestone occasions and a wonderful way to remind the guest of honor how celebrated he or she really is. Let your honoree's unique personality influence the style and theme of your party, and the details will fall into place.

You can host a birthday party any year, but the big milestones—30, 40, and 50 (or the years just before the big 0's)—are the most popular for blowout birthday bashes. And they're especially exciting if you make the party a surprise!

First, decide on the kind of party you want to have. Almost anything works at a birthday event, but dinner parties or "drinks/appetizers/dessert" get-togethers are the most popular. You might want to try something different for your celebration—host an early-morning breakfast, surprise picnic, or "progressive dinner party" with surprises at each home (see the Comings and Goings Parties chapter on p. 99 for details on the progressive dinner party).

Here are some ideas for hosting a one-of-a-kind birthday party for your one-of-a-kind guest of honor:

- Design your party around the honoree's vocation. Have your guests dress up as "patients" for a doctor, "students" for a teacher, "fellow scientists" for a computer engineer, and so on. Decorate to suit the theme, with eye charts, X rays, and stethoscopes for the doctor; pencils, books, and maps for the teacher; and pen packs, flow charts, and taped glasses for the computer engineer.

- Focus your party around your special guest's hobby, and have everyone dress as famous detectives for the mystery buff, athletes for the armchair quarterback, or famous celebrities for the movie lover.

- Host a party with the special guest's favorite activity as the main event. Go to a football game, horse race, bowling alley, or fashion show.

- Throw an "over-the-hill" party, with parodies of growing older. Many party goods supply stores have products for this theme, but you can make your own black armbands, create personalized tombstones, and arrange for an on-duty "nurse" to care for the guest of honor throughout the party.

- Try a "Middle Ages" theme. Feature costumes, food, and decorations from the days of King Arthur and Camelot to poke fun of someone who has finally reached middle age.

- Have a "back-to-high-school" party, and hold the birthday bash at the honoree's high school gym, if possible. Invite old friends to shout out cheers, sing the school song, and dance all night. Decorate the walls with memorabilia from the guest of honor's teenage years to take a walk down memory lane.

- If it's a big birthday milestone, host a *big* birthday party with oversized decorations and large gifts, such as a keg of beer, crate of bubble bath, or carton of sweets.

Here are some fun party ideas that can be adapted to suit any theme:

- Gourmet picnic at a local park.
- Fish fry—guests bring their own "catch" to grill on the barbecue.

- Ice skating or skiing party.
- Entertainment party with a comedian, fortune-teller, or singer.
- Road rally for bicyclers.
- Nostalgia dinner in a local diner or "dive."
- Floating party in a houseboat, sailboat, or other small craft.
- Ethnic party, such as an Italian spaghetti feed, Mexican fiesta, or Caribbean night.

Many hosts like to make their birthday parties a surprise. If that's your plan, be sure to get an assistant to help keep the guest of honor in the dark and out of the way until the party begins. Here are some ideas for pulling it off:

- Take the guest of honor out to dinner, and have your assistant welcome the guests. When you return from dinner—surprise!
- Ask the guest of honor to get the babysitter across town. When he or she arrives there, have the sitter's parent explain there's been a mix-up and the sitter had already been driven to the home. This gives you time to let your guests in and set up for the party.
- Take the guest of honor out to dinner, but get halfway to your destination and remember you forgot something, such as your wallet. Have the guests waiting at a neighbor's house, ready to move into your home when you leave. When you return home, go in for the forgotten item while the guest of honor waits in the car. Pretend you can't find the item, and ask for help in the search. When the guest of honor gets in the house, have everyone shout out, "Surprise!"
- Invite friends to assemble at a restaurant. When you and the guest of honor arrive, have everyone stand up and yell, "Surprise!"
- Plan a surprise lunch with a group of friends, and make everyone wear T-shirts that say "Happy Birthday, (Name)!"
- Hold the party at a friend's house, if the guest of honor is a family member. That way the guest of honor won't see the decorations or get suspicious.
- Have the party a few days before or a short time after the

official birth date.

- Throw an early-morning or late-night surprise party to catch the suspicious one off guard.

- Plan a surprise party for a friend who has an actual or imaginary birthday near the birth date of the real guest of honor, and then turn the tables on him or her—the honoree has helped plan his or her own surprise party!

- Have all the guests meet at a neighbor's house, gather all the food and props, and then walk en masse to the guest of honor's house and ring the bell—surprise!

Invitations

Birthday invitations can be created from anything appropriate to your theme. Here are a few suggestions you might want to consider:

- Photocopy a birth certificate or old birth announcement on parchment paper for your invitations, adding your party details instead of the birth details.

- Photocopy pictures of the guest of honor as a baby (or an adult), mount them on colored tagboard, and write your party details underneath them.

- Draw a simple birthday cake on a colorful tagboard card, and write your party details around it. Tape a small birthday candle on top of the cake, wrap the card in tissue to protect it, and mail.

- Write your party details on a colorful square of tagboard, and wrap the invitation with birthday gift wrap. Or take this idea a step further, and drop the card into a small gift-wrapped box.

- Get a copy of the front page of a newspaper from the day and year your birthday guest was born, and photocopy it. (You can write to the newspaper of your choice and ask them for a copy—most will send a photostat of the front page. Or try the library.) Cut out one of the articles and substitute your own, beginning with a headline about the guest of honor's birth and following with details about the party. (If you have a computer, you can make up a realistic column.) Photocopy your paste-up, and mail it to your guests. For added fun, you might ask your guests to dress up in the style of the year the honoree was born.

- Hire an artist to draw a caricature of the guest of honor, and use photocopies for your invitations.
- Write your party details on a party horn or party hat.
- Photocopy a calendar sheet on colored paper and mark the date of the party on the calendar, with party details.
- Cut out the horoscope section from a newspaper or magazine, and substitute a typewritten horoscope predicting the birthday party, with the party details written underneath.
- Put confetti inside your invitation envelopes, and seal them with a birthday sticker.
- Choose some aspect from your special theme, such as a picture of a fish for a fish fry, and write your party details on the back.
- For a vocation-theme party, send invitations on prescription sheets for the doctor, report cards for the teacher, computer graphs for the engineer, or on other vocation-related items.
- For a "back-to-high-school" party, write your invitations on sheet music that doesn't have any words. Title your song invitation "Sixteen Candles," and then cross off the "Sixteen" and write in the age of the guest of honor. Add your party details where the words should be, photocopy the sheet music invitation, and mail it to your guests.
- For a "back-to-high-school" bash, ask your guests to come dressed as they did in high school. Here is a sample invitation you might want to use as a model:

> Hey all you beboppers and mo-taters, jocks and dorks, hoods and rah-rahs, and even you cheap dolls with bad reps. It's (Name's) 40th birthday (280 in dog years) so we're turning the clock back to (date of party), 1959, when virgin pins were more valuable than Rolex watches, letter sweaters more coveted than stock options, and easy girls more popular than political scandals. Put on your poodle

skirts and dungarees, grease your D.A.'s, put your hair in a pony-tail, cover your zits and hide your ciggies, and bebop down to (name of high school) to show everyone how to be cool in the rock-and-roll '50s.

- If you're throwing a surprise party, the best way to invite your guests is to call them—that way there's no evidence lying around for the honoree to discover. Stress the importance of being prompt.

- For a "Middle Ages" party, cut out a sword from silver paper, write your party details on it, and stick the sword in an envelope. When your guests pull the sword from the envelope, they'll feel just like King Arthur pulling the sword from the stone. Be sure to tell everyone to come dressed as Lancelot, Guenivere, Merlin the Magician, or another knight or damsel.

- Ask your guests to write a funny poem or anecdote and bring it along to use during the roast or videotape activity on p. 58.

- If your party has an "over-the-hill" theme, send a black balloon or black invitation, include black armbands, and suggest to your guests that they dress in mourning.

- Write the details of your surprise party on an inflated balloon with a permanent ink, felt-tip pen. You might add a line like, "Shhh . . ." or "Don't Blow It!" Deflate the balloon, and stick it in an envelope with instructions to blow it up.

Balloon Invitation

Decorations

Create a festive atmosphere for your birthday party, using some of the following ideas:

- Fill your party room with colorful streamers, confetti, and balloons. You might want to create a gazebo effect by attaching different-colored streamers to the middle of the ceiling, draping them out toward the walls, and letting the ends hang down. Or hang a large balloon or paper ball in the center of the room, and drape paper curls over it. Sprinkle confetti on the tables and floor, and hang balloons from the ceiling.

- Fill a closet with balloons, and ask the guest of honor to retrieve a miscellaneous item from it—watch the look of surprise when the balloons tumble out!

- During the party, fill the honoree's car with balloons as an extra surprise.

- Hire a few members of a high school band to play "Happy Birthday" during the party.

- Collect items from the guest of honor's baby book or the year of his or her birth, and turn them into a centerpiece for your table.

- Line the walls with pictures of famous people born the same day as the birthday guest. You can find this information at the library in various almanacs and get the pictures from magazines, record stores, or art and poster shops.

- Find the day's horoscope in a newspaper, and copy it onto a large sheet of tagboard. Or make up a funny one of your own.

- For old folks who think young, pick out a line of paper products with a youthful theme, such as Mickey Mouse or Barbie plates and cups, or baby shower items that feature cute babies.

- Fill the party room with helium balloons (they'll float to the ceiling) and dangling colored ribbons. Fill the balloons with helium at a party goods supply store, or rent a helium tank so you're not breathless when the party starts.

- If you have a "This Is Your Life" theme, place a photograph timeline along one wall to chronicle the honoree's life from birth to the present. Mount the photos on silver stars, and add funny captions underneath. Cut out silhouettes of "mystery guests," and hang them on the wall. Decorate the whole room with stars.

- Black should be the color scheme at your "over-the-hill" party. Cover the table with a black paper tablecloth and use black plates, napkins, and cups. (Many party goods supply stores carry a line of "over-the-hill" paper party products that should delight your guests.) Place the gag gifts in the center of the table, with two black candles on either side. Blow up black balloons and hang them from the ceiling. Greet the guest of honor with a wheelchair, and dress his or her spouse in black.

"Over-the-Hill" Decorations

- To decorate for a vocation-theme birthday party, just pick out items that fit the guest of honor's career. Create a doctor's office with wall charts, X rays, a list of contagious diseases that are going around, lots of candy pills, educational charts about the human body (available from teacher's supply stores)— even a fake dead body covered with a sheet! Play music appropriate to the vocation, such as "Dem Bones" for the doctor, educational songs from "Sesame Street" for the teacher, and electronic/synthesized music for the computer engineer.

- For a "back-to-high-school" party, you can create a high school in your own home if you can't rent the gym of your old alma mater. Decorate the walls with posters of classic rock stars, such as Elvis and Ricky Nelson, Beaver Cleaver photographs (available at movie memorabilia stores), old record album covers, cut-outs of records from black and white construction paper, and sheet music of songs from the rock-and-roll era. Any artifacts from the '50s or '60s would be appropriate, such as real Coke bottles or old saddle shoes.

  Hang up photos of the guest of honor from past to present, and write funny captions under each picture. You might want to decorate the party room with a high school prom theme, such as "Under the Sea" or "Enchanted Evening." A great idea is to rent a juke box (see your Yellow Pages under "Juke Boxes"), and the company you rent from will try to supply you with any songs you request. Then let your guests play their favorite tunes all night.

- Make your "Middle Ages" party room look like a set from *Camelot*—an old castle or atmospheric forest. Rent the movie to get ideas about what to re-create. With a little paint and paper, you could have your guests in Camelot by nightfall! Play the music from *Camelot* throughout the party, or take a break from Richard Harris and play some Gregorian chants or medieval folk music.

Games and Activities

Here are several "ageless" games and activities you can use to add sparkle and fun to your birthday party:

- If you've created a timeline with photographs of the guest of honor, assign a picture to each guest and have them write a funny comment. When everyone is finished, have the guests read their comments.

- Turn your birthday party into a "Roast." Provide a long

banquet table to seat your guests, with a special spot in the middle for the "roastee." Rent, borrow, or make a podium and allow each guest to stand up and relate a funny story, recall a nice memory, or tell an amusing anecdote about the guest of honor. For funny lines and any-occasion roast ideas, look for *The World's Funniest Roast Jokes* by Red Stangland (Meadowbrook Press, 1992).

"Roast" Party

- Take your guests aside during the party, and videotape them relating a funny anecdote or poem about the honoree. Play the tape during the party, and give it to the guest of honor as a gift.
- Sometime before the party, make a videotape of still pictures chronicling milestones in the honoree's life. Add a funny story line to go along with each picture, pausing for several minutes at each one. Play the tape at the party.
- Have each guest bring a wrapped memento from some event they've shared with the honoree. It might be a broken ski from a disastrous ski trip, a shirt with a wine stain from a wild party, or a theater program from a fun night on the town. Have each guest explain the significance of the gift as it's opened.
- Hire an electronic message company or skywriter to write "Happy Birthday" in the sky.
- Quiz a relative or good friend about embarrassing moments in the honoree's life, and write each one on a piece of paper. At the party, have each guest pick a slip of paper and act out the

embarrassing moment. Have the guest of honor try to guess what's happening.

- Dig out a few interesting facts about the honoree—an unusual hobby, an odd middle name, or a secret fantasy—and write them on slips of paper. Then make up several strange facts that are *not* true about the person. At party time, mix up the true and false facts, pick one, and read it aloud. Ask the first person on the left to tell whether it's true or false. Give a cheap gag gift to anyone who guesses correctly.

- If you're hosting a "This Is Your Life" birthday party, you'll need to prepare ahead of time. Contact some special friends and relatives that your guest of honor hasn't seen in a while, and invite them to be "mystery guests" at the party. Ask them to bring along a poem or funny anecdote about the honoree. Make silhouettes of their heads on black paper (with a white question mark inside each silhouette), and tape them around the walls. Then tape-record their poems or stories and hide the mystery guests in another room.

  After the honoree arrives, begin the "This Is Your Life" activity. Holding a large book with pre-written notes inside, tease your birthday star with a few clues to the identity of the first mystery guest. Then play the tape recording. Allow time for the honoree to guess, and then bring out the mystery guest.

- For a vocation-theme party, play games appropriate to the guest of honor's career. If your guest of honor is a doctor—well, you can't play doctor—but you can play the "Prescription Game" where all the guests prescribe good luck or success to the guest of honor in unique ways. If the honoree is a teacher, play "Trivial Pursuit" to test everyone's knowledge. If you're honoring a computer engineer, collect an assortment of technical terms and computer jargon from a specialty dictionary or reference book, and have everyone guess what the words mean.

  Or play "Liar's Trivia." Do a little research on the guest of honor's vocation or hobby, digging out unusual facts and questions. At party time, ask your trivia questions, and have the guest of honor give answers that might be true or false— make sure he or she lies convincingly! Have the first person to the guest of honor's left verify or deny the answer by saying, "I agree" or "I disagree." Give a cheap gag gift to anyone who guesses correctly.

- For a "back-to-high-school" theme, play a "Name That Tune" game with pre-recorded bits of songs from the past. Many radio stations play oldies you can tape, or you can buy some oldies collections at a record store. Have a dance contest featuring dances like the Twist, the Mashed Potato, and the Swim. Write down old TV show quotes such as, "Gee, Wally!" from "Leave It to Beaver" or "Waaah, Ricky!" from "I Love Lucy," and see if your guests can name the show.

- In the Middle Ages they used to play drinking games, so a "Middle Ages" party is a good place to have a wine tasting. Ask your guests to bring a favorite bottle of wine, with the label covered by a paper bag. Give everyone a score sheet and pour the various wines throughout the night, asking guests to guess and write down which kind of wine they are drinking. Keep track of the winners, and award a good bottle of wine as a prize. (As an alternative, you can award a prize to the guest who brought the most flavorful wine—have your guests vote for their favorites.)

Refreshments

Most birthday parties feature a large decorated sheet cake from the bakery—it's simple, makes a nice centerpiece, and feeds a crowd without a lot of hassle. However, you might also want to provide munchies and drinks. Here are some fun party-food suggestions:

Theme-Party Foods

- Have a bakery make a unique cake that ties in with your theme, such as a design that features the guest of honor's vocation, hobby, or interests—a textbook, giant baseball, or sailboat, for example.

- For a "back-to-high-school" party, ask a bakery to create a giant "hamburger" cake. This certain-to-be-popular cake looks like an enormous hamburger with all the trimmings. Or have a cake made in the shape of a record album with the guest of honor's name as the label. Serve hamburgers, hot dogs, and other junk food items, or try old-time favorites such as tuna casseroles, Jello, Moon Pies, and ice cream sodas.

- A "Middle Ages" cake could resemble a sword or other item from that time period. Or have a bakery create two cakes shaped like the guest of honor's age, such as a big "4" and "0" to symbolize middle age.

Homemade Cakes

- If you want to make a stunning birthday cake on your own, try this: Buy a chocolate cake mix, or prepare one from scratch. Pour the mix into a large sheet cake pan. Spoon in a can of cherry pie filling, and swirl it through the batter. Then bake as directed. Top your cake with whipped cream and maraschino cherries.

- Buy or bake a large chocolate sheet cake and separate it into three layers after the cake has cooled, using a bread knife or dental floss. Cover the first layer with whipped cream and sliced strawberries, and then top it with the second sheet cake layer. Cover that layer with whipped cream and sliced strawberries. Top it with the third layer, cover it with whipped cream, and decorate the top with small, whole strawberries. Drizzle fudge topping over the whole cake and serve. Delicious!

- Instead of having a traditional birthday cake, you can make an ice-cream (or frozen yogurt) cake. Buy or bake a sheet cake in the honoree's favorite flavor. Separate the cake into two sheets when cool, using a bread knife or dental floss. Using a rectangular, half-gallon carton, slice the ice cream or frozen yogurt into $1/2$-inch thick slabs. Place the ice cream or frozen yogurt between the cake layers—to avoid smashing the bottom layer of cake, either freeze it before putting on the ice cream or slightly melt the ice cream layer before stacking. Return the cake to the freezer while preparing the frosting.

Buy or make frosting in your guest of honor's favorite flavor. Frost the cake quickly, and return it to the freezer until serving time. Top it all off with strawberries, cherries, chocolate curls, flaky coconut, or chopped nuts, and serve immediately.

- Make a cake that is lower in sugar by preparing a sugar-free angel food cake or shortbread and covering it with berries and whipped cream.

Other Refreshments

- Serve champagne—at least for the toast or while serving the cake. Then you can switch to wine or a sparkling punch.
- Have munchies on hand for your guests. Flavored popcorn is a great crowd-pleaser and is easy to prepare. Pop the kernels according to package directions, drizzle with butter, and mix in one of the following: Parmesan cheese, lemon-herb seasoning, Mexican seasoning, dry sour cream seasoning and onion salt, or powdered Cheddar cheese.

Prizes, Favors, and Gifts
● ●

Your "Best Party" birthday celebration will be memorable with the following extra touches.

Prizes and Favors

Party-game prizes and favors can be silly or serious. Here are some to try:

- T-shirt, bumper sticker, or pin that reads, "(Name) is 40" or "I'm a Friend of (Name)."
- Tickets to a play or movie (perhaps with the host as escort).
- Cookbook or a book about entertaining.
- Coffee mug with a saying about friendship or a book about friendship.
- Bottle of wine with the guest of honor's personalized label.
- Tin of cookies.
- Gourmet items like coffee or chocolate sauce.
- Poster of the guest of honor blown up from a photograph.
- Plant or bouquet of dried flowers.

- Apothecary jar filled with jelly beans.
- Vocation-related prizes such as candy pills, decorated pencils, or pens.
- High school-related prizes—an old 45 record, a poster of Elvis, or a pack of bubble gum.
- Middle Ages-related prizes—a bottle of grog, a turkey leg, a sword toy or letter opener, or a copy of Chaucer's *Canterbury Tales*.

Gifts

If you or your guests are looking for special gift ideas, consider giving the guest of honor presents that celebrate the wonderful friendships he or she has made over the years. Or try gifts that are just plain silly and fun. Consider some of the following ideas:

- Items symbolizing a past experience together would be appreciated and treasured by the guest of honor. For example, if you attended a Mozart symphony together, pick up a copy of the movie *Amadeus*, or if you vacationed together in Hawaii, give a poster of Waikiki Beach.
- Address book with friends and relatives listed.
- Box of fine cigars or candies.
- Tickets to a sporting event.
- Blank videotapes or a videotape of a favorite movie.
- String of lottery tickets equal to the honoree's age. For example, if it's a 40th birthday, give forty lottery tickets.
- T-shirt for someone who's turning forty that says, "Just turned 30." (Be sure it's ten years younger than the real birthday!)
- New piece of sporting equipment to keep the honoree in shape—a basketball, tennis racket, barbell, or jump rope.
- Box full of gourmet foods—a jar of caviar, gourmet popcorn, decadent fudge sauce, fancy olive oil or vinegar, and specialty teas and coffees.
- A star named after the guest of honor: For about $40, the International Star Registry will name a star after someone, and send him or her a frameable registration sheet, the location of

the star, and a map of the constellations. You can take the honoree outside, point toward the heavens and say, "Guess what? I just made you immortal." For more information, call (800) 282-3333.

- If the honoree is turning eighty or older, you can have the President send a special birthday card to him or her—send a birthday request (including name, address, and occasion) four weeks ahead of time to: Greetings Office of the White House, Washington, DC 20500.

Gag Gifts

The subject of aging is ripe for jokes, and everyone has a good laugh as the guest of honor tears the gift wrap off his or her new collection of anti-aging aids. If you or your guests need ideas, consider some of the following:

- Denture cleanser (for that new set of choppers).
- Foggy mirror (to make those wrinkles "disappear").
- Toothless comb (for the gentleman who's "losing it").
- Fan (for hot flashes).
- Magnifying glass or large-print book (for failing eyesight).
- Tube of Detane (for men only).
- Granny shoes (for those tired feet).
- Grecian Formula (for those distinguished-looking gray hairs).
- Baby food (for those with no teeth).
- Cane.
- Subscription to *Modern Maturity*.
- Copy of *The Joy of Sex* by Alex Comfort (Crown, 1972).
- Bottle of Geritol or iron tablets.
- Pair of bifocals from the Goodwill.
- Brochures from a local cemetery.
- Jar of Porcelana.
- Copy of *How to Survive Your 40th Birthday* by Bill Dodds (Meadowbrook Press, 1990).

- Senior-citizen-discount bus application.
- Birthday control pills—a little medicine bottle filled with jelly beans and labeled, "Birthday Control Pills: Take one, once a year, to control birthdays."

Theme-Related Gifts

- For a vocation-theme-related gift, consider a book about the guest of honor's vocation or an appropriate "tool of the trade."
- For a high school-related gift, try a hair-care kit with comb and Brylcream (or hair spray), some old 45s, or a blow-up poster of the guest of honor's high school photo.
- For a Middle Ages-related gift, offer dinner at a Steak-and-Ale restaurant or a hair-coloring kit, false teeth, or other gag gift related to old age.

Chapter 6

It's truly a cause for celebration when a couple shares a milestone anniversary. The couple gets a chance to renew their love—perhaps even their vows—and your guests get to share the joys of that enduring love.

There are generally two types of anniversary parties. You can host an anniversary party for you and your partner, and perhaps ask your friends to bring "memories" and special mementos rather than gifts. Or you can host an anniversary party for a couple celebrating a number of years or decades together. Here are some suggestions for anniversary party themes:

- Try re-creating the original wedding (or if the couple eloped, creating the wedding they never had), complete with an authentic wedding cake, photographer, and even a minister or justice of the peace. This could be a fun surprise party.

- Bring back the "good old days," when your guests of honor were young and newly in love, by providing music, decorations, and food from their courtship years. The Big Band sound, bebop, or even the music of the Beatles can suggest a theme for the party and create an atmosphere that represents the time the couple was married.

- Host a community party where everyone chips in and rents a cabin or a block of hotel rooms in a nearby resort town. It's fun, easy, and different. The money contributed for the party can also be used for cleanup, which makes for an easy finale. And everyone gets a romantic weekend away!
- See the Wedding Shower chapter on p. 11 for more romantic anniversary celebration ideas.

Any anniversary year may be celebrated, but the big ones—1st, 5th, 10th, 20th, 25th, and 50th—are the most popular milestones. You might want to use traditional or modern anniversary themes for your party—or embellish them a bit to fit your personal style. Here's a list of traditional and modern themes for easy reference:

WEDDING ANNIVERSARY GIFTS/THEMES

	Traditional	Modern
First	Paper	Clocks
Second	Cotton	China
Third	Leather	Crystal/Glass
Fourth	Fruit/Flowers	Appliances
Fifth	Wood	Silverware
Sixth	Candy/Iron	Wood
Seventh	Wool/Copper	Desk Sets
Eighth	Bronze/Pottery	Linens/Laces
Ninth	Pottery/Willow	Leather
Tenth	Tin/Aluminum	Diamond Jewelry
Eleventh	Steel	Fashion Jewelry
Twelfth	Silk/Linen	Pearls
Thirteenth	Lace	Textiles/Furs
Fourteenth	Ivory	Gold Jewelry
Fifteenth	Crystal	Watches
Twentieth	China	Platinum
Twenty-fifth	Silver	Silver

WEDDING ANNIVERSARY
GIFTS/THEMES (continued)

	Traditional	Modern
Thirtieth	Pearl	Diamond
Thirty-fifth	Coral	Jade
Fortieth	Ruby	Ruby
Forty-fifth	Sapphire	Sapphire
Fiftieth	Gold	Gold
Fifty-fifth	Emerald	Emerald
Sixtieth	Diamond, yellow	Diamond, yellow
Seventy-fifth	Diamond Jubilee	Diamond Jubilee

Invitations
●●●●●●●●●●●●●●

You might find appropriate invitation ideas in the Wedding Shower chapter on p. 13. Here are some other unusual and creative ways to invite guests to your anniversary party:

- Purchase some plastic champagne glasses, and write the names of the celebrating couple on them—many craft stores sell a liquid "silver" you can use for writing on them. Write your party details on the bottom or opposite side of the glass. Tie a small white ribbon around a wisp of artificial flowers or bells, and secure it to the stem of the glasses. Mail them in a small box, or hand-deliver.

- Cut out two double hearts from red tagboard, and write your party information inside. Punch a small hole at the top of the hearts, and tie on red or white ribbon.

- Cut out two doves from white tagboard, and write your party details on the back of them. Connect the doves with a thin strand of white ribbon, and drop them in an envelope filled with a bit of white confetti.

- Buy small bride and groom figurines at a bakery or party goods supply store, and tie a card with your party details to them.

- Cut out pictures of famous lovers from magazines, and glue them around a piece of colored construction paper. In the center of the paper, glue a photo of the celebrating couple. Draw speech bubbles above all the famous lovers, and put your party information inside the bubbles. Make photocopies for all your guests.

Couples Invitation

- Write out a marriage certificate on parchment paper, filling in your party details instead of wedding details. Roll it up, and tie it with white and red ribbon. Mail it in a cardboard tube.

- Design your invitations to look like an actual wedding invitation, and have them printed up at a professional print shop. This type of invitation is especially classy for a 25th or 50th wedding anniversary.

- Borrow photographs of the celebrating couple as a young bride and groom and as they are today. Make photocopies, and use the bride-and-groom photo for the front of your invitation and the contemporary photo on the inside with your party details.

- Buy postcard reproductions of Grant Wood's *American Gothic*, and write your party details on the back of them.

If you're going to host an anniversary party using traditional themes, you might want to try some of these invitation ideas for milestone anniversaries (modify them to fit the "modern" themes, if you wish):

- 1st Year: Print up invitations on fancy paper, or make unique invitations out of tissue-paper flowers. Mail them in a small box with paper confetti, or hand-deliver.

- 5th Year: Write your party details on small wooden cutouts or decorations shaped like wedding bells, hearts, or doves (available at most hobby stores). They can be painted or decorated to suit your theme.

- 10th Year: Wrinkle up a piece of aluminum foil, smooth it out again, and wrap the foil around a small heart-shaped piece of cardboard. Then color the foil with a wide felt-tip marker, and write the party information with a permanent ink, felt-tip pen.

- 15th Year: Send invitations on white tagboard cards covered with pearlized paper. Attach a small crystal bead (available at most hobby stores) to the card with nylon thread, and tell your guests the crystal is for "good party karma."

- 20th Year: Playing on the "china" theme, send invitations written on rice paper, a Chinese fan, or small Chinese paper lantern. If you can find someone who knows Chinese, have them write the invitations. (Be sure to include a translation!)

- 25th Year: Have all party information printed on silver paper, and then glue the paper onto cardstock. Cut the invitations into bell shapes, and send them to your guests.

- 50th Year: Send gold-embossed invitations. For a special touch, tie two imitation wedding rings to one corner of the invitation with gold thread.

Decorations

Create a romantic atmosphere for the celebrating couple. Here are some ideas for making your party room more romantic:

- Cut out red hearts from tagboard or construction paper, and hang them from the ceiling with red ribbon. Or hang white doves and lovebirds from the ceiling with white ribbon.

- Buy or rent pots of flowers and plants to fill your party room with blossoms and greenery. Tie large pink, red, and white bows around the pots.

- Have a photograph of the celebrating couple enlarged, and hang it on the wall. Ask some of their friends and relatives about important dates in the couple's life, and write them down on heart-shaped cards—then surround the photograph with the cards. Make a line, using colored yarn, from the photograph to each of the cards to create a history of the couple's romantic past.

- Make a decorative timeline of the celebrating couple's marriage, with pictures gathered from family and friends. Line the photos along one wall, with romantic or funny captions underneath.

- Re-create the couple's courtship period with items reminiscent of their younger days. Make copies of old newspaper headlines from the day they met and the day they were married. Hang photographs of the celebrating couple as young lovers. Have your guests dress in the style of their courtship years, and play music appropriate to that era.

- Spray paint your centerpiece with silver or gold paint to make it look dazzling for the silver or gold anniversaries. Or just give it a sweep with the spray paint to gild the edges.

Here are some ideas for decorating with traditional themes (modify them to fit the "modern" themes, if you wish):

- 1st Year: Decorate the party area with paper flowers, paper tablecloths, fancy paper plates and napkins, a paper centerpiece, and paper accessories.

- 5th Year: Decorate with wooden plaques, use wooden bowls and serving pieces for the food, set the food on wooden tables or barrels, and paint your guests' names on wood scraps for place cards. Send wood favors home with your guests— chopsticks, wooden plaques with funny sayings, and pencils.

- 10th Year: Cover your table with aluminum foil. Use metal

serving utensils and containers, and decorate with silver accessories such as candlesticks, knickknacks, and candy bowls. Make a centerpiece out of tin food cans: Tear the labels off, and write funny clues about what's inside with a permanent ink, felt-tip pen. Offer the can collection to the guests of honor as they leave—for "mystery" meals to eat later on. Give your guests small gifts or favors made from tin, aluminum, or other metals. Wrap all prizes, gifts, and favors in aluminum foil.

- 15th Year: Rent, borrow, or use your own crystal to serve food and drinks. Hang small crystals from the ceiling, and fill crystal bowls with "crystal" candy (available at candy stores). Set a mystical crystal ball on the table for a fortune-teller (see p. 77 for more details). Send your guests home with fancy sugar crystals that come in a variety of colors (available at coffee and gourmet foods stores).

- 20th Year: Use Chinese accents throughout your party room, such as Chinese lanterns and vases, incense, and Chinese art reproductions. Serve Chinese food on your best china. Send

"China" Theme Decor

everyone home with a homemade fortune cookie that has a personalized fortune inside.

- 25th Year: Use only silver serving pieces, if possible—you can rent them from a party goods supply store. Hang silver stars and bells from the ceiling, and decorate with silver tinsel and accessories. Serve dessert topped with tiny silver bells (available at confectionery or bakery supply stores). Send everyone home with silver earrings or cufflinks, or faux silver items.

- 50th Year: Fill the room with golden-colored flowers (daffodils, mums, or yellow roses). Cover your table with gold paper gift wrap, and put a lace tablecloth over it. Hang imitation wedding rings, gold stars, or gold bells from the ceiling. Serve food on gold serving pieces, if available (if not, wrap some platters in gold foil). Offer gold-foil-wrapped chocolate coins alongside a fancy dessert. Send everyone home with gold coins, gold pens, or personalized gold trophies.

Games and Activities

A version of "The Newlywed Game" from the Wedding Shower chapter can be a fun activity for your anniversary party (see p. 19 for directions). Another fun and creative game is the individually-designed "Personal Trivia Game." It takes some work ahead of time, but it's well worth the effort since it will make your party unique.

For the "Personal Trivia Game," write trivia questions pertinent to the group of friends attending your party. You'll be amazed at the things you don't know about your friends—perhaps you'll learn more than you care to know! Here's how to play: Several days before your party, call each of your guests and ask them some questions about their background. Tell them not to discuss the questions or answers with anyone. If you're inviting a large group (eight or more), jot down about fifteen questions and answers per person—if it's a smaller group, you'll need even more questions and answers per guest. Cut some brightly colored paper into small cards, and write the questions on one side of the cards and the answers on the other. Shuffle the cards before you begin the game.

Depending on the size of the group, divide up into teams or play individually. You can use a "Trivial Pursuit" board or simply go around the room drawing cards, asking questions, and keeping track of points. If it's your turn to read a question, look at it first and make sure it's not a question about the person or team who must answer (they will obviously know the answer—that's no fun). Just replace that card and select another. *Note:* You, as the host, will know all the answers since you wrote all the questions. Nevertheless, it's great fun watching the group struggle for answers, make mistakes, and laugh at the surprises.

Here are some trivia questions to get the game started. Just look at the question by "Phone" so you know what to ask your guests, and then translate it into a trivia-type question like the ones by "Card." Fill in the appropriate names and pronouns where necessary.

1. Phone: What were you doing when you met your spouse?

    Card: When (Name) met (name of spouse), (he/she) was working as:
    (a) a forest ranger, (b) a census taker, (c) a lion-tamer, or (d) a belly dancer.

2. Phone: What's the most unusual job you've ever had?

    Card: Which one of us actually worked as a grave digger?

3. Phone: Have you won any awards in the past or received some kind of honor for something?

    Card: Which one of us carried the title, "Miss Hog Caller of 1978"?

4. Phone: Where did you meet your partner?

    Card: Where did (Name) meet (name of spouse)?
    (a) at McDonald's, (b) in a men's room, (c) at the unemployment office, or (d) over a CB radio.

5. Phone: Where did you go on your first date?

Card:	Where did (Name) take (name of spouse) on their first date? (a) (his/her) apartment, (b) (his/her) bedroom, (c) the backseat of (his/her) car, or (d) home to mother.
6. Phone:	Where did you spend your most unusual vacation?
Card:	Who in this crowd spent three weeks at a fat farm?
7. Phone:	What are your pets' names?
Card:	Who has a pet goldfish named Jaws?
8. Phone:	What was your maiden name?
Card:	Who was formerly known as Miss Bilgebottom?
9. Phone:	Where did your "first time" take place?
Card:	Which one of us "did it" for the first time on the Space Mountain ride at Disneyland?
10. Phone:	What is your pet name for your partner?
Card:	Who in this room is usually referred to in private as Snookie-wookie-poo?
11. Phone:	Where were you born?
Card:	Which historical site does (Name) claim as (his/her) birthplace? (a) Muscogie, IL, (b) Gorky Park, Russia, (c) Burbank, CA, or (d) Ellis Island.
12. Phone:	What was the strangest adventure you've ever had?
Card:	Name the person here who escaped from a Russian gulag.

If you're having a traditional-theme party, try some of these game and activity suggestions (modify them to fit the "modern" themes, if you wish):

- 1st Year: Play a pencil and paper game or a board game that is appropriate for couples, such as "Scruples," "The Dating

Game," and "Love Connection." Have guests make funny paper hats for the celebrating couple, and award a prize to the winner for best hat. You might also make a "money tree" centerpiece or decoration using dollar bills, and have your guests of honor answer personal or trivia questions for each buck.

- 5th Year: Play a game that uses wooden tiles or pieces, such as "Jenga," "Cribbage," or "Scrabble." Have your guests build a creative structure out of wood chips for your guests of honor to take home and set on their mantle or coffee table.

- 10th Year: Have each guest bring a few canned goods (with the labels removed) for the celebrating couple. Tell your guests to write cryptic clues on the cans with a permanent ink, felt-tip pen so the couple can try to guess what they'll be eating for dinner next week.

- 15th Year: Invite a fortune-teller to your party (or have a friend dress up and play medium). Have him or her use a crystal ball to read the fortunes of all your guests, with special emphasis on the future good fortune of the celebrating couple.

- 20th Year: Hire a professional to write all your guests' names in Chinese on a decorative card, with an explanation of each name in English on the back. Offer everyone a homemade fortune cookie with a special personalized fortune inside.

- 25th Year: Have each guest name a phrase, song, or book that has the word "silver" in it, such as "Hi-Oh, Silver," "Every Cloud Has a Silver Lining," "By the Light of the Silvery Moon," and "Silver Anniversary," until everyone is stumped.

- 50th Year: Have each guest give the celebrating couple a gold-foil-wrapped chocolate coin, and offer with it a memory of or a special wish for the couple.

Here are some other fun activities to consider for your anniversary party:

- Have everyone bring a photo of the celebrating couple, along with an amusing story. Mount the photos on the wall, and at game time ask each guest to tell an anecdote about the couple. Place all the photos in an album after the party to give to the guests of honor.

- Videotape all your guests relating the story of how they met the celebrating couple and sharing a special memory about them. Play it back for the crowd during the party, and give it to the couple as a gift.

- Ask each guest to bring a personal trivia question for the happy couple that relates to some past experience. For example, if a guest went on vacation with the couple, he or she might ask, "What happened in Fresno on July 19, 1977?" If the couple can remember, award a small prize—perhaps a gag gift.

- Borrow slides (secretly!) from the couple's personal collection, and pick out some of the funniest ones. At party time, give a slide show and ask the couple to explain each scene. Or present your own funny version of what's happening in the slide.

Refreshments

Many of the refreshments suggested in the Wedding Shower chapter on p. 22 are appropriate for your anniversary party. Here are some more suggestions for simple and delicious treats:

- Make a stunning (and edible) centerpiece with a miniature wedding cake—it will bring back fond memories for your guests of honor and serve a crowd! This type of cake doesn't have to be expensive if you keep it simple, small, and elegant.

- Fill cream puffs with white chocolate mousse for a special treat.

- Fill a graham cracker-crust pie shell with a small carton of thawed-out frozen raspberries. Then cover the berries with your favorite non-bake cheesecake filling, and top with a chocolate sauce that will harden when refrigerated. Decorate with whipped cream rosettes and fresh raspberries.

- Serve pink champagne or a fruit punch with the fancy desserts.

For more traditional anniversary refreshments consider the following (modify them to fit the "modern" themes, if you wish):

- 1st Year: Serve all the food on paper products, and offer paper-wrapped chicken (a Chinese specialty dish available at Chinese restaurants) as a main course.

- 5th Year: Serve your refreshments on wooden serving pieces, and offer chopsticks.

- 10th Year: Present your food on metal plates and bowls, and use metal utensils.

- 15th Year: Use crystal serving pieces, and serve crystalized candy with your dessert.

- 20th Year: Serve Chinese food (make your own or get take-out) on your good china.

- 25th Year: Serve everything on silver, and use tiny silver dragées (edible candy balls) to decorate your desserts.

- 50th Year: Rent or borrow some gold serving pieces if you don't have any of your own, or cover your serving dishes with gold wrap. Serve gold-foil-wrapped chocolate coins.

Prizes, Gifts, and Favors

Anniversary parties need special touches to add flair, romance, and fun to the festivities.

Prizes

If you have game winners, try some of these prizes:

- Small game of trivia.
- Romantic tape or CD.
- Small bouquet of flowers.
- Romance novel.
- Bottle of pink champagne.

Gifts

If your guests need gift suggestions, refer to the traditional (or modern) theme list for a starting point, or try one of these:

- 1st Year: Stationery printed with the celebrating couple's names, a romantic book about marriage, or a reprint of the newspaper from the day they were married. (You can write to the newspaper of your choice and ask them for a reprint copy—most will send a photostat of the front page. Or try the library.)

- 5th Year: Wooden serving pieces, wooden napkin rings, or a wooden picnic basket.
- 10th Year: Cans of food with the labels removed, metal serving pieces, or a metal appliance.
- 15th Year: Crystal serving pieces or champagne glasses, "crystal" candies, or crystal knickknacks.
- 20th Year: China serving pieces, china figurines, or Chinese art reproductions.
- 25th Year: Silver serving pieces, silver jewelry or cufflinks, silver picture frames, or silver decorative items (silver-plated, faux silver, or real silver).
- 50th Year: Gold serving pieces, gold pens, or gold decorative items (gold-plated, faux gold, or real gold).

You might also recommend the following gifts:

- Romantic dinner-for-two gift certificate.
- Sexy nightwear.
- Theater tickets.
- Tickets for a local boat cruise, hot air balloon trip, or a hansom cab ride.
- Basket of wine, cheese, and French bread.
- Romantic tape or CD, and massage oil.
- A night-on-the-town gift certificate (for dinner, drinks, dancing, or entertainment).
- Bottle of pink champagne.

Favors

Send your guests home with some romantic party favors:

- Single red rose.
- Small corsage.

- Bubble bath or fancy soaps.
- Bottle of champagne.
- Bouquet of silk wildflowers.

Chapter 7

Whether it's a high school graduation or a celebration of that college degree, you won't need a lot of pomp and circumstance to host a fun, final farewell to school days. Here are some suggestions for honoring the graduate that will be as memorable as the school years themselves.

Invitations

Send your guests some special invitations to get your bash started. Just study the following invitation suggestions, and make your selection—it's multiple choice!

- Write your party details on crisp white paper in a calligraphic style (as if the invitation were a diploma), roll up the paper, and tie it with ribbons in the graduate's school colors.

- Make mortarboard invitations. To do this, buy some black envelopes, write your party details on white cardstock, and insert the cardstock in the envelopes. Take a long strip of black construction paper, cut wide fringe along one long side, bend

83

it into a circle to form the base, and glue it onto the back of the sealed envelope to make the "hat." Attach a tassel—homemade from black felt or purchased from a hobby and crafts store—and hand-deliver.

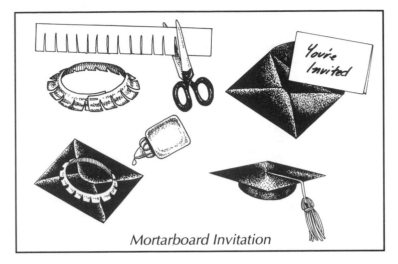

Mortarboard Invitation

- Make a copy of the school mascot on a sheet of paper, and write your party details above it. Get creative, using inspiration from the mascot. For example, if your team is called the Wolves, add some wolf prints; if they're called the Mustangs, add a picture of Mr. Ed; or if they're called the Knights, draw a few swords or a grail.

- Make an invitation that looks like a final exam. Word it to give your guests a chuckle as they read their "test." Here's an example:

  1. If you were going to (Name)'s graduation party, would you want:

     a. Lots of food?

     b. A disc jockey?

     c. A toga party?

     d. All of the above!

Continue with these multiple choice questions, and fill in your party details at the bottom of the invitation. You could even make the invitation look like a "blue book" by folding over light blue paper for the front and back cover and pasting notebook paper containing your exam questions on the inside.

- Make your invitation look like a report card. Photocopy a real report card, and add your own party details to it. You might even personalize each invitation for your guests, giving some of them bad grades and some of them good!

- Use college brochures as invitations, especially ones from Ivy League colleges or unusual places like Mortician's College or College of Taxidermy. Or make your own recruitment brochures for your invitation using construction paper, a typewriter or computer, and a little creativity.

- Make elegant invitations from quality paper using the school colors—one color for the paper and the other color for the envelope. Have the invitations professionally printed, with an imprint of the school logo on the front.

- Photocopy a kindergarten or elementary school photo of your guest of honor, and write your party details on the reverse side. Or photocopy his or her senior picture to use on the front of the invitation. You might also find a picture of the school the guest of honor is graduating from, photocopy it, and draw a large red circle around it with a red line through the center over the school.

- Ask your guests to dress up for the party. You can either ask them to dress formally or dress stereotypically as cheerleaders, jocks, nerds, greasers, teachers, and so on.

Decorations

You've probably saved a few school mementos over the years— now they'll come in handy as decorations for your party room. Here are some suggestions for re-creating the school atmosphere:

- Decorate with lots of rolled up diplomas and mortarboards made from black construction paper and felt (or real) tassels. Set them on tables, hang them from the ceiling, or use them as a centerpiece. Write a special message inside the diplomas for each guest, and use the diplomas as place settings.

- If your school mascot (usually a costumed student) lends itself to partying, include him or her—or it—at the celebration. Perhaps you can borrow the real one from the school—costume and all—to help lead the cheers, or make your own mascot costume with a little creativity.

- Get out all your mementos from high school and college, and use them as a centerpiece for the table. You might include such items as dance tickets, dried-up corsages, prom photos, textbooks, and old reports, projects, or papers.

- Display all your honoree's school yearbooks so your guests can browse through them during the party. Photocopy yearbook pictures of guests who will be attending the party, and hang them on one wall of your party room.

- Photocopy and enlarge some yearbook photos of favorite or not-so-favorite teachers to admire, deface, or write funny comments on.

- Cut out want ads from a newspaper, photocopy and enlarge them, and arrange them on poster board with circles and arrows pointing to the strangest jobs, as omens for the future. You might include such occupations as "Busboy," "Bundle Spotter," "Forklift Operator," "Process Server," or "Time Share Salesperson."

- For a high school graduation party, hang banners and pennants from a number of colleges.

- For a college graduation party, put up want ads or brochures from large corporations.

- Rent a few movies that deal with high school and college to play in the background, such as *Rock-and-Roll High School, Fast Times at Ridgemont High,* or *National Lampoon's Animal House.* You might also play some high school or college-oriented music—marches, fight songs, the soundtrack from *Grease,* or a local college radio station, if possible.

Games and Activities

Your guests will probably spend most of their time talking about school and remembering old times, but here are a few party games to play before the final bell rings.

What's That Teacher's Name?

This game might sound easy, but it's not! Your guests can probably name most teachers and professors by their last names, but what about their first names? Using a yearbook for the answers, have the gang take turns trying to remember the first names of different teachers, professors, deans, custodians, and especially those of the principal or president.

Where's That College Located?

Using the encyclopedia or another reference book (e.g., a guide to colleges), find some names of famous colleges or universities. List them on a piece of paper and read each one aloud, having your guests name the city and state where the colleges or universities are located. Again, this game is more challenging than it sounds!

School Trivia

Play a trivia game using the academic questions from "Trivial Pursuit"—"History," "Arts and Literature," and "Geography," for example. Hold a "Trivia Bee" where guests have to stand up to answer questions. Keep a tally of questions answered correctly, and award a prize to the "student" who answered the most.

School Daze

Go through your old school-year calendars, and write down some special dates on which major events occurred. You might include the senior prom, the first day of summer vacation, the day the English teacher was fired, the first day of school, Homecoming, Freshman Orientation, and so on. Read only the dates—day, date, and year—and have your guests try to remember what happened that day.

Whatever Became of . . .?

Photocopy your guests' yearbook pictures, and glue them onto individual sheets of paper. Give one picture to each guest at random, and have him or her write down a funny future prediction in the form of "Whatever Became of . . .?" For example, "(Name), captain of the football team, became the proud owner of his own drop-in brain-surgery clinics throughout the state," or "(Name), former drama student, became the spokesperson for all the Kmart Blue Light Special announcements." Have each guest read his or her own caption to the group, for silly and embarrassing results.

Refreshments

Refreshments are easy at a graduation party—as long as you have enough! Just for fun, try some of the following suggestions:

- Serve typical cafeteria food (only better) in the traditional school style. If you can borrow or rent some serving trays, all the better. Serve the food cafeteria style, with lines of food along a table or counter, and have "cafeteria helpers" dole it out. (You can have your helpers wear aprons and hair nets for an added laugh.) Put the name of each dish on a little card beside it—make labels that read "Meat Surprise" or "Broccoli Jello" to remind your guests of the institutional food they'll never have to eat again.

"Cafeteria" Refreshments

- Serve the food in lunch boxes. If you've saved your own from your school days, great. If not, borrow a few from some neighborhood kids or use regular lunch bags.
- Offer the usual junk food favorites, such as a variety of pizzas

delivered from various pizza joints, hamburgers with tons of toppings, or a giant poorboy sandwich from a deli. Keep the sodas (and beer, if your guests are of age) flowing, and be sure to have plenty of potato chips, dip, and raw vegetables to snack on.

Prizes, Gifts, and Favors

Have your party graduate to a higher level of fun and festivity. Try some of the following ideas:

Prizes

- Pencils emblazoned with the school name.
- Pen set for future academic or occupational use.
- Pennants or banners with the school team or motto on them.
- Dictionary or thesaurus.
- "How to get a job"-type books.
- Key chain symbolizing the key to the future.

Gifts

- Weekend vacation—all expenses paid.
- The *Fortune 500* book, or a subscription to *The Wall Street Journal* or *Entrepreneur* magazine.
- Dishes, bedding, and cleaning supplies for that new apartment.
- Personalized license plate (from your county or state's license information center) with a message like: GETAJOB (Get a job), NOMOSKL (No more school), FREALAS (Free at last), GRADU8 (Graduate), TIM2WRK (Time to work), or CPA2B (CPA to be).
- Disks or other items for a home computer (or a computer or electronic typewriter, if you can afford one!).
- Funny tie or other symbol of the job world.

Favors

- Pencils, rulers, or other school supplies.
- Address books for keeping in touch.
- T-shirt or sweatshirt with the school name on it.
- Photos of the whole gang.
- Apples for future teachers or bosses.
- Mugs that say "Class of 19XX."
- Copy of the week's want ads.

Chapter 8

Everyone dreams of the day he or she will get to walk out the office door, having said goodbye to the boss for the last time. It's the thought of retirement that keeps a lot of us going, so when it finally happens—celebrate!

If you're the one who's turning in your time card, you can plan a party for yourself and celebrate with friends, relatives, and former co-workers. Or if you're planning the party for someone special who's looking forward to a life of leisure, here are some suggestions for creating a memorable "last day."

Invitations

There are several ways you can invite the office crowd or friends to your retirement party. Personalize the invitations to fit the retiree and set the tone for the party. Try one of these invitation ideas to get the party started:

- Using a paycheck as a model, type up an imitation paycheck to mail to your guests. Fill in the date of the party where you would normally put the date on the check, fill in your guests' names in the space provided, and sign your name where the check normally requires a signature. Then fill in your party details in the open space on the check. Write something like, "Good for one evening of fun and good cheer" on the line where the amount is usually written. Use your imagination to personalize the invitation and make it humorous.

Paycheck Invitation

- Write up a fake resume for the retiree, with funny descriptions of odd jobs he or she has had over the years—include PTA officer, neighborhood tool-lender, and so on. Make the last entry on the resume "Guest of Honor" and write your party details underneath.

- Pick up some brochures from a local retirement community, and fill in your party details on each one. Or create your own humorous, personalized brochure, and write the party information inside.

- Send your guests cruise or vacation brochures from a travel agency, to symbolize the retiree's new life of leisure, with your party details included.

- Write your party details on any item that relates to leisure time, such as motor home brochures, hobby instruction sheets, and golf course ads.

- Design a newspaper headline declaring the day of your party a national holiday due to the retirement of a special person. Make newspaper columns that outline the place, time, and date of the party. For laughs, include a photo of your guest of honor's head, and place it on a body (from a magazine or retirement brochure) wearing a goofy tourist getup or leisure outfit. Or include a "before and after" advertisement for stress management or cosmetic surgery from a magazine, with a caption like, "working versus retired."

- Send each guest an inexpensive white sailor cap with your party details written on the inside. On the outside write, "Gone Fishing—Permanently," to intrigue the guests. If you can't find sailor caps, write your party details on a handmade fishing license, and attach an inexpensive lure (no sharp points!).
- Ask your guests to come dressed as stereotypical retirees—in leisure suits, tourist outfits, fishing gear, housecoats, T-shirts, golf clothes, and beach togs.

Decorations

Setting up your party room to look like a retiree's dream is as easy as picking up that final paycheck. Here are a few suggestions:

- Tie up a small hammock made from fishing net or other netting to hold the guest of honor's gifts. Or set up a "retirement scene" with a real hammock, hat, radio, tropical drink, newspaper, and pillow. You might even want to stuff some clothes to create a retiree in effigy.

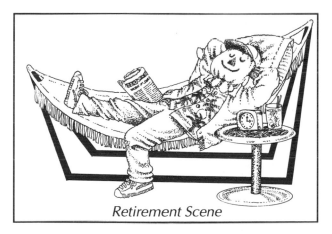

Retirement Scene

- Hang up posters and brochures from retirement communities, cruise ships, distant ports of call, airlines, and railways. If the retiree is planning a special trip, use it as a theme for your decorations.

- Use the guest of honor's unique hobby or activity as a central focus for the party. For example, if the guest of honor is a golf fanatic, set up golf clubs and balls in a display or centerpiece, have everyone wear golf clothes, hang golf tees from the ceiling, put up posters of famous golfers, and rent a "how-to-golf" video to play in the background. If the hobby is painting, set up easels, spread out tubes of paint on the tables, hang up prints by famous artists, or have the guests bring one of their own homemade works of art to display for artistic "inspiration."

- If the retiree is undecided about how to spend the "golden years," decorate your party room with lots of suggestions. Include sports equipment, travel destinations, or even some want ads for classic retiree jobs, such as "Security Guard," "Newspaper Deliveryperson," or "Fast-Food Server"—enlarge them, and hang them on the wall with job tips.

- Display pictures of the guest of honor as he or she appeared at work over the years. Or set out memorabilia from significant accomplishments on the job, such as a picture of a building he or she designed, a sample of a product he or she produced, or a life-saving piece of equipment he or she used in an emergency.

Games and Activities

Usher in the retiree's new phase of life with a fun-filled party. Consider these suggestions:

- Have a "This Is Your Life" ceremony for the guest of honor. Invite co-workers and friends to say a few words about incidents that occurred at work, and let the retiree guess who's speaking before revealing his or her identity.

- Hold a roast, giving all the guests a chance to poke fun at the retiree. Everyone will enjoy hearing funny stories about the special guest (as long as the anecdotes aren't mean-spirited). You might also have everyone share stories about their most embarrassing moments with the retiree.

- Play "Check Your Retirement Quotient." Ask each guest to test the guest of honor's retirement "aptitude" by asking questions about possible retirement plans and having him or her demonstrate leisure skills. Have the guest of honor show everyone how to swing a golf club, dance a current dance, tie a fly-fishing lure, cook a meal with four pre-selected ingredients, or pronounce a few French phrases.

- Ask each guest to write down a suggestion for a leisure-time activity. Most of your guests will probably write something funny or silly, such as, "Finally learn to program the VCR," "Return my lawnmower," or "Write that sexy romance novel you've been wanting to write—but only after you've had some real-life experience," and so on.

Refreshments

The refreshments can be simple, implying the impending cut in wages, or lavish, in celebration of job accomplishments over the years. Try some of these ideas:

- Simple "poor bum" refreshments might include pork 'n' beans, bologna sandwiches, and corn bread. (Just be sure everything still tastes good.) Serve the food on paper plates, with lots of mismatched glasses.

- For first-class refreshments, you might want to have the party catered by a local restaurant or catering service.

- If the retiree is planning to take a trip, serve food related to the destination, such as Mexican food for a trip to Mexico or Italian for a flight to Rome.

- If the retiree usually took a bag lunch to work, hand your guests brown paper bags filled with surprising gourmet refreshments. Your guests will have fun opening the lunch bags and finding hot fajita pockets or elegant pasta dishes, instead of the usual boring peanut butter and jelly sandwich. Wrap all the food in plastic wrap, too.

- Have a bakery make a special cake or centerpiece for the retiree, using work or leisure as a theme. The cake can be designed in the shape of a house for a retiring architect, a cash register for a clerk, or a briefcase for a businessperson. If the theme is leisure, create a cake that looks like a golf course for a golf fanatic, an open book for an aspiring writer, or a boat for a sailing enthusiast.
- Serve champagne for toasting the success of the retiree. Then serve beer or non-alcoholic beverages for the rest of the party.

Prizes, Gifts, and Favors

Everyone will have fun showering the retiree with best wishes. Here are some ideas to help make the party extra-special:

Prizes

- Bottle of champagne.
- Deck of cards.
- Retirement, leisure, or hobby magazines.
- Badminton or croquet set.
- Humorous book about retirement.

Gifts

- Materials appropriate to the retiree's hobby.
- Mementos from work, such as a special desk calendar, file, or computer accessory.
- Tickets to the theater.
- Foreign-language phrase book for the retiree's vacation plans.
- Book with suggestions on what to do when you're bored, or a retirement guide.
- Hammock.
- Sports equipment.
- Favorite tape or CD.
- Six-pack of beer.

- Subscription to *Reader's Digest*.
- Decorated blank book for starting that novel or personal journal.
- Leisure shirt, sweat suit, or other comfortable piece of clothing.
- Photo album filled with pictures of co-workers and work-related mementos.

Favors

- Cheap "gold" watches.
- Inexpensive pen sets.
- Plastic ball and chain from a novelty store.
- Fancy lunch bag.
- Antacids (note that antacids and other favors are for those who still work at the same old grind).

Chapter 9

In this highly mobile society, we all see a lot of friends come and go. The best thing to do when old friends leave or new ones come into our lives is to throw them a party they're not likely to forget. Here are three types of parties for welcoming the "new" and saying good-bye to the "old."

MOVING AWAY PARTY

A "movable feast" or "progressive dinner" is a great theme for a moving away party. Ask three other guests to help host the party by having part of the progressive dinner in their homes, and then divide the evening into quarters. Begin with drinks and hors d'oeuvres at one house, and move on to the next house for soup and salad. Allow plenty of time for everyone to eat their fill, but warn people not to eat too much because there will be two more stops. Go to the third house for the main course, and wrap up the evening at a fourth home with dessert, after-dinner drinks, and coffee.

Be sure to plan your feast with three hosts who live near one another so there isn't too much travel time. Car pool if possible to keep the party full of energy and to allow friends to continue their conversations. If alcohol is going to be served at any of the stops, ask your guests to select designated drivers before the party begins—or hire a limousine to transport your guests from house to house.

Invitations

Gather your guests for a big going-away party with one of these "moving" invitations:

- Make invitations from baggage claim tickets (they're available at most airline terminals). Or design your own tickets from tagboard and colored paper.

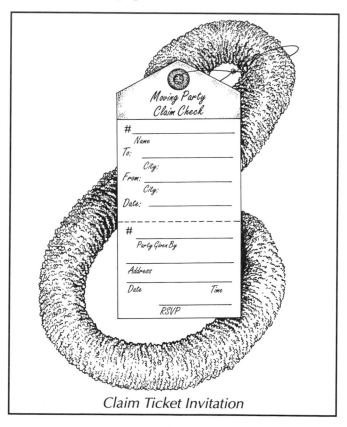

Claim Ticket Invitation

- Dig up some old airline tickets, block-out the airline information, and fill in your party details. If you can't find old tickets, you can make your own from tagboard.

- Send for travel brochures from your local Chamber of Commerce, and write your party details on the inside of them.

- Include information about a progressive dinner if you're having one, and be sure to state whether it's a surprise.

- Ask your guests to send or bring some memorable photos from past events—the ski weekend, the camping trip, or the yearly Halloween party—then put the photos in an album, write some funny captions, and present it to the relocating guest during the party.

- Ask each guest to bring the name, address, and phone number (and a photo, if possible) of someone they know in the guest of honor's new city. The lucky "mover" will then have several new contacts.

- Ask your guests to dress up for the party in outfits that parody the place the guest of honor is moving to. For example, if the guest of honor is moving to a sunny state like California or Florida, have people dress stereotypically in Hawaiian shirts, sunglasses, and sandals. If the weather at their destination is likely to be different from what they're used to, have people dress in the type of clothing the "mover" will probably be wearing a lot—raincoats (for a move to Seattle), ski outfits (for Alaska), or swimsuits (for Miami). With a little creativity on everyone's part, you might have a room filled with Hollywood starlets, Dallas cowboys, or Iowa farmers.

Decorations

Your moving away party will be fun and stylish with a few special touches:

- Outline the guest of honor's destination on a large sheet of tagboard. Use an atlas, and mark down all real or imaginary points of interest on the tagboard. Most states have several odd-sounding towns that can be marked with a thumbtack. Tape one end of a piece of yarn near the thumbtack, and pull it out toward the wall. Tape funny descriptions of the towns to the other end of the yarn. On construction paper, write your phony descriptions of the places—"Paris, Texas . . . Not exactly an 'eyeful.' " "Amityville, New York . . . A 'spirited' city." or "Naughtright, New Jersey . . . Home of Murphy's Law."

- Having your guests dress up will help provide atmosphere, so have some T-shirts made with special slogans such as "New Jersey or Bust," "California, Here I Come," or "I ♥ New York." Or get a T-shirt displaying the city or state of destination—most cities and states offer T-shirts with their names emblazoned on the front (you can mail-order them from a T-shirt shop). You might also have T-shirts made up with the name of the city or state your guest of honor is leaving. Then ask the T-shirt makers to superimpose a red circle with a line through it over the picture of the old hometown. Include the name of the city or state of destination beneath it.

- Make a centerpiece containing items that symbolize the area the guest of honor is moving to. Use a ten-gallon hat for Texas, a variety of cheeses for Wisconsin, or a bowlful of pasta for Italy. Joke gifts are fun, too—a rubber worm in an apple for New York City, for example.

- Make place settings from flags representing the new state or country your guest of honor is moving to, and use the state or country colors for your color scheme.

- If your guest of honor's destination suggests any particular type or piece of music, play it in the background during the party. For example, if the honoree is headed for New York, play "New York, New York," or if he or she is going to Tennessee, play plenty of country and western music.

Games and Activities

Try these games and activities to help celebrate your guest of honor's new life in a new home:

- Play a game of "Where the Heck is Hackensack?" This is a game everyone should enjoy, whether they're headed for a new locale or not, but it will take a little research before the party. Find a few books at the library about the guest of honor's destination. Dig up thirty to forty obscure facts about the area, and jot them down on a piece of paper. At game time, read the questions aloud and give everyone a chance to write down the answers. Here are a few examples, using the state of New Jersey:

1. What's New Jersey's nickname?
2. The New Jersey state insect is the:
   (a) bumblebee, (b) honeybee, or (c) killer bee.
3. What is the title of the New Jersey state song?
   (a) "Born to Lose," (b) "Itsy-Bitsy, Teeny-Weeny, Yellow Polka-Dot Bikini," (c) Theme music from "60 Minutes," or (d) None.
4. Which state boasts the birthplace of Lou Costello, John Forsythe, and Ozzie Nelson—California or New Jersey? (For this type of question, give your guests a choice of two states—the one the guest of honor is moving from and the one he or she is moving to.)

Read over the answers, and give a prize to the guest who got the most correct.

- Wrap up a bunch of items for the move, and pack them in a suitcase. Include such things as maps of the new town, stationery for keeping in touch, flashlights in case there's no electricity, water jugs in case there's no water, and items to help the "mover" acclimate, such as suntan lotion for a move to a tropical area or mittens for a cold climate. Have the guest of honor unwrap each item one by one while everyone watches.

- Have your guests write down the worst moving experience they ever had. Give the anecdotes to the guest of honor, and have him or her read them aloud. Once everyone stops laughing, give each guest a chance to offer a bit of "moving" advice.

- Give your guests a geography lesson. Distribute paper and pencil to the group, and have everyone draw an outline of the mover's new state or country and pinpoint the guest of honor's new city or town—all in only five minutes time. Hold up each drawing, and have everyone vote on the winner—

award a prize to the winning guest. This game will really take everyone back to the fifth grade!

- Give the guest of honor a "survival kit" full of stationery, chocolate chip cookies, a mug with a saying about friendship, and other mementos to help him or her survive in an unfamiliar place. Have the guest of honor open the kit in front of everyone.

Refreshments
• • • • • • • • • • • • • • • • • • •

Memorable moving away parties offer guests a variety of taste treats. Here are some ideas you can try:

- A progressive dinner needs a lot of organization ahead of time. Decide how many courses and homes will be involved, and then assign them in geographical order, to make travel time minimal. Four homes and four courses usually works best.

  Begin with hors d'oeuvres and drinks at one home, and hand out your maps there. Continue with soup and salad at the next home, asking everyone to bring along some cut-up vegetables and a favorite dressing. Move on to the third house for the entree. A fun entree suggestion is Pesto Linguine. You need: 2 cups fresh basil, $\frac{1}{2}$ cup olive oil, $\frac{1}{4}$ cup chopped pine nuts or walnuts, $\frac{1}{2}$ cup grated, fresh Parmesan cheese, 2 tablespoons grated Romano cheese, 2 pounds fresh linguine, 3 tablespoons butter or margarine (melted), and 2 tablespoons water. Place the fresh basil in a blender with olive oil and nuts. Whirl the mixture on high speed until it's blended. Pour it into a bowl, and stir in Parmesan and Romano cheeses. Cook the fresh linguine in rapidly boiling water for 3 minutes. Drain, and place it in a bowl. Add the melted butter and water to the pesto, and stir it into the linguine. Serve immediately.

  Wrap up the evening with dessert in the last home. Chocolate fondue is always fun, and everyone can chip in by bringing apples, mini-marshmallows, nuts, pretzels, snack food, caramels, bananas, and other favorites for dipping. To make chocolate fondue, melt 8 squares of semisweet baking chocolate and 1 tablespoon of butter in a saucepan, over water, or in a microwave. Pour it into a serving dish or heated fondue pot, alongside the fruit, nuts, and candy.

- For a special treat, bake a cake in the shape of the guest of honor's new state, and decorate it with assorted lakes, rivers, mountains, earthquakes, volcanoes, quicksand, and other features—real or not.

Prizes, Gifts, and Favors

Try these ideas so your guests and guest of honor won't be leaving the party empty-handed:

- Poke fun of the fact that the guest of honor is "leaving" everyone by having the guests wear specially made buttons that read, "I'm *not* from New Jersey" (or whatever the destination).
- Present game winners with guidebooks to the guest of honor's new city or state.
- Give gifts that stereotype the "mover's" destination, such as oversized items for Texas, sunglasses for California or the tropics, foreign-language books for overseas, or big apples for New York City.
- Give the guest of honor plenty of stationery, along with self-addressed, stamped envelopes. Add an address book, too. Make it easy to stay in touch!
- Present the guest of honor with some local wines to help toast the gang in absentia (and forget his or her sorrows).
- Have a nice photograph of the guest of honor's old house taken, or hire an artist to draw a picture of it. Ask all your guests to chip in a little money to get it framed.
- Give the guest of honor a one-year subscription to his or her old newspaper to help ease the transition from one place to another.

HOUSEWARMING PARTY

If you're hosting a housewarming for a newcomer to the neighborhood or for an old friend relocating to the area, have your guests bring a favorite dish (perhaps from their native area) for a potluck. A surprise party works well for a housewarming, too.

Invitations

Welcome your guests to a housewarming party by sending out a special notice:

- Have an artist or friend draw a sketch of the guest of honor's new house. Photocopy it, fold it into a card, and write your party details inside.

- Cut out a mailbox shape from colored tagboard (folded in half so the invitation will open up along the fold line), and write the guest of honor's new address on it. Open the invitation, and write your party details inside. Or make single-thickness mailboxes, cut a slit where the door would be, and stick in a small "letter" (with party details) that can be pulled out.

- Find a picture of a tumbledown shack and photocopy it, telling your guests (for fun) that it's the guest of honor's new home. Write your party details on the back of the picture.

- Using a map, photocopy the route taken when the guest of honor moved. Write your party details on the back.

- Tie a yellow ribbon around your invitation to symbolize a welcome home.

- If your housewarming party is going to be a surprise, mention this on the invitations.

Decorations

Set a "Best Party" mood for your housewarming guests—here are some ideas to try:

- Tie yellow ribbons of welcome on the doors, chairs, tables, and other items inside the house, and even on the trees, mailbox, and lamp post outside.

- Photocopy sections of a map of the community, town, city, or state to use as place mats.

- If your guest of honor is new to the area, hang a map on the wall with useful points of interest—the best grocery store, the cheapest gas station, the most popular restaurant—it's decorative and helpful. If the guest of honor is just relocating within the community, you can use the map to point out the most unusual spots of interest—use your imagination.

- For a newcomer to the area, pick up some samples from various local stores, and use them as a centerpiece. Buy croissants from your favorite bakery, coffee from a gourmet store, or meats from a good deli.

Games and Activities

Break the ice and introduce the newcomers to the neighborhood with any of the following party-pleasers:

- Give your guest of honor a "guided tour" of the area. To do this, take slide shots or make a videotape of various local "highlights" beforehand. Jot down a few humorous notes so you can narrate while giving the "tour" during your party. At party time, delight your guests with local sites like the city dump (while boasting about the "luxurious and prestigious neighborhood") and the local biker bar (while promising a "great night life").

- Introduce everyone at the party, giving a brief description of each person's occupation, family, and so on, and then give the guest of honor a quiz on all the new information. Or give the guest of honor a list with each guest's name, occupation, hobby, and other personal details, and have them guess who's who.

- Write up some funny true or false questions about the area, and quiz the guest of honor. Appropriate questions might include these "true or false" items:

1. The name of the local high school is Elvis Presley High.
2. The population of the town is 408 (unless there's a baseball game in the city).
3. The festival queen is called "Miss Zucchini."

Make sure some of the questions are true and some false, but have fun with it—the more ridiculous the true answers, the better.

Refreshments

Fill your home and party room with the wonderful aroma of tempting food:

- Have a potluck, and request that each guest bring a specific dish. If it's a brunch, you'll need drinks (orange juice, Bloody Marys, champagne, and coffee), bread (rolls, croissants, pastries, and bagels), meat (bacon strips, ham slices, and sausage links or patties), and perhaps a fruit dish or salad. You might also want to serve a dessert.

- Ask your guests to bring a recipe along with the food item, or to bring the food item in a nice basket, plate, or dish to give the new homeowner.

- Have your guests bring food from the newcomer's former area for a potluck. For example, if the guest of honor moved from Texas, people can bring items for a barbecue; or for a newcomer from Florida, Southern fried chicken and lots of oranges. This gesture will make the guest of honor feel at home.

Prizes, Gifts, and Favors

Housewarming gifts and other mementos come in many shapes and sizes. Here are a few suggestions:

- Items fitting for a "household tree"—a hammer, screwdriver, bolts, and a tape measure. Make a wooden tree from scrap lumber, and then tie on much-needed tools for the newcomers.

- Housewarming plant.
- Sample item from a favorite store. For example, a salad from the grocery store deli or flowers from a favorite greenhouse or flower shop.
- Frozen meals—if each guest brings one to the party, the guest of honor will have a stock of dinners to last for a while.

BON VOYAGE PARTY

Most people take a vacation now and then, and sometimes it's the dream trip they've been saving up for—a cruise to Alaska, a tour of Europe, two weeks on a tropical island, or a climb up a Himalayan mountain. If you have a friend who's heading out of town, throw him or her a surprise bon voyage party, and design the theme around the destination point.

Invitations

Say good-bye in a major way—gather the gang together with the right invitation:

- Find some postcards that represent the vacation spot, and send them to your guests. For example, if the tropics is the destination, pick out pictures of beaches; if it's Disney World, send out pictures of Mickey Mouse.
- Write your party details on a baggage claim ticket (available at most airport terminals), and tie the ticket onto an inexpensive item that represents the vacation spot. For example, send a plastic lei if a Hawaiian vacation is planned, or an apple if New York City is the destination.
- Write your party details on travel brochures advertising the specific vacation spot.
- If the guest of honor is headed for a foreign country, write the invitation in the language of that country or region (be sure to provide a translation!).
- If the party is to be a surprise, mention this in the invitation.

- Ask your guests to dress for the vacation spot. Have them wear kilts for Scotland, safari-wear for Kenya, or Mickey Mouse ears for Disneyland. Or just have everyone come dressed as tacky tourists, complete with loud shirts, cameras, sunglasses, and even suitcases.

Decorations

Set the scene for a dream vacation with the following decoration tips:

- Hang a colorful map of the vacation spot. (You can give it to the guest of honor as a gift after the party.)
- Hang posters and pictures depicting the vacation spot.
- Set up your party room to look like an airplane, cruise ship, or scene from the vacation spot. Greet your guests in flight-crew or nautical uniforms (borrowed, rented, or makeshift), and play Muzak. Or rent an "in-flight" movie to play in the background.

Vacation Scene

- Arrange items relating to the vacation destination as a center-piece—pineapples and fish nets for Hawaii; a teapot, teas, and cakes for England; and sunglasses and suntan lotion for California.

Games and Activities

Don't let your guest of honor leave home without getting into one of the following activities:

- Collect brochures from a travel agency, and cut out destination "clues" to glue onto poster board. Have your guests guess each destination from the clues on the brochures.

- Have each guest relate their worst vacation experience.

- If your guest of honor is going abroad, borrow or buy a traveler's phrase book, and write down some foreign-language phrases. Ask everyone to write down their translation of the phrase, and read the answers aloud. Have fun with this by picking out funny phrases, such as the following German examples:

  "Es kommt kein warmes Wasser." ("There's no hot water!")

  "Darf ich Sie nach Hause bringen?" ("May I take you home?")

  "Ich mochte etwas gegen Reisekrankheit." ("I'd like something for travel sickness.")

  "Rufen Sie schnell einen Arzt." ("Call a doctor quickly!")

Encourage your guests to give creative responses.

- Prepare a "survival kit" for your guest of honor before the party—your guests can bring items to make this a fun group activity. Fill up a suitcase with wrapped vacation-survival items, such as plug adapters; Dramamine; a foreign-language phrase book; self-addressed, stamped postcards; maps; film; and freeze-dried snacks.

Refreshments

Your bon voyage bash will be just the right send-off with good food and drinks. Serve the kind of refreshments or meal that the guest of honor might get while on vacation. For example, if Mexico is the destination, have a Mexican fiesta dinner with margaritas, enchiladas, burritos, tostadas, and flan; serve a Polynesian dinner for the vacationer headed for the tropics, baked Alaska for an Alaskan cruise, or sukiyaki for a trip to Japan.

Prizes, Gifts, and Favors

Send the vacationer—and the rest of your guests—off into the wild blue yonder with one of the following traveler's aids:

- Travel guidebooks.
- Magazines.
- Puzzles.
- Small travel games.
- Best-selling novel.

Chapter 10

Reunions are a great way to gather together long-lost relatives, old friends and neighbors, service buddies, school chums, sorority sisters and fraternity brothers, and former co-workers—any collection of people who haven't seen each other for a while.

Reunions call for special planning, since many of the guests may no longer live close-by. As host, you might have to make arrangements for the out-of-towners at local hotels, or clear out a large room for sleeping bags and overnight guests. This, along with the numerous tasks involved, might seem overwhelming. The best way to make it easy on yourself is to ask another reunion member who lives nearby to help out with party planning and cleanup. The more help you get, the easier your reunion will be.

Here are some suggestions for putting together a special reunion for your friends or family:

- Set up individual committees if your reunion is going to be large. For example, if you're hosting a family reunion, assign each attending family a reunion task. Divide the work into about six basic categories, and assign the tasks to various groups as shown in the following list:

1. Have one group create and photocopy the invitations, directions, and maps. They might also help with accommodations for out-of-town guests (see the Invitations section in this chapter).

2. Have a group prepare the house or party site by decorating and setting up chairs, tables, and place settings (see the Decorations section in this chapter).

3. Have a group organize and buy the food (keeping in mind the theme and style of the party) and collect money from guests, if appropriate (see the Refreshments section in this chapter).

4. Have a group prepare, heat, and serve the food (see the Refreshments section).

5. Have a group select and organize the games, activities, and entertainment (see the Games and Activities section in this chapter).

6. Have a group organize cleanup and trash removal, and generally get the party site back in order.

- The style of your reunion will influence the planning. You might want to host a picnic or potluck—they work best with most reunion parties since they're casual and easy to set up and clean up. You might want to have the groups get together ahead of time to prepare the food as a team, or have everyone bring their individual contributions the day of the party.

- Consider hosting the reunion at a central location—at a place that's convenient for the majority of the guests—and then have everyone stay at the same hotel. Or host your party at a local park, making preparation and cleanup easier on everyone. End the gathering with a pancake breakfast in the park the day before everyone heads home.

- If you host reunions on a regular basis, you might assign a theme each time. Perhaps one year the theme could be "Memories," and everyone could bring a past memory about another reunion member. Another year you might want to focus on "Reacquaintances," and just let everyone get to know one another again.

Other ideas for themes include: "New Members" (a focus on the introduction and welcome of new family members through marriage or birth); "What's New?" (a theme to bring everyone up-to-date on recent accomplishments and activities); or "Predictions" (everyone can predict the future for other reunion members and then check back at the next reunion to see which predictions came true). Or pick out a general theme such as a ski party, a *Gone with the Wind* party, a Texas-style barbecue, a "Roaring Twenties" bash, a toga party, a murder mystery party, a clambake, or a "tacky" party (see the More Excuses for a Party chapter on p. 205 for more general party themes).

Invitations

There are lots of ways to create unusual reunion invitations to send to your relatives, neighbors, or school pals. Try some of these suggestions for your family, old neighborhood, or school reunion:

Family Reunion

- Photocopy a picture of your family, and fold it into a card. Write the details of the reunion inside.

- Collect a photo of the oldest family member and the youngest. Cut them out, and tape them to a folded sheet of paper to make a card. Unfold the paper and photocopy it, and then refold it and write your reunion information inside. If you find a photocopier that does double-sided copying, write your party details inside first, and then photocopy. You might mention something about getting everyone together, from "granny" to "baby."

- Cut out a tree trunk from brown construction paper for a family tree. Glue it onto a white sheet of paper, and write your party details around the tree in green ink for "leaves."

- Make a detailed family tree with the names of each family member as leaves. Put question marks for missing information about relatives and ask family members to fill in the blanks, and bring them along to the reunion (or call them ahead of time, and fill in the missing details before the party begins).

- If your family has a sign or symbol, such as a coat of arms or crest, or if your family's last name has another meaning, such as Blackstone or Nightingale, design your invitation to look like it. Write your party details on the back.
- Photocopy a genealogy chart, and use it as the cover for your invitation.
- Draw a 5-by-5-inch quilt pattern, and use it for your invitation. Ask each family to create a quilt square symbolizing their family, and bring it along to the reunion (see the Games and Activities section in this chapter for more details).

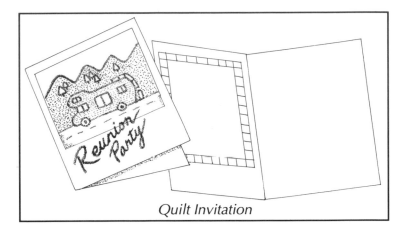

Quilt Invitation

- Make a miniature family photo album from tagboard, and write the reunion information inside.
- Make "secret pal" invitations. To do this, assign one family member to be the secret pal of another family member and prepare some "surprises." At the reunion, the special pals should exchange treats, notes, small gifts, and mementos. It's especially nice if a young person and older person are assigned to each other (but don't assign the same people to each other).
- Cut out or draw a map of your state or region, photocopy it, and glue it onto a card. Draw a line from your city or town to the edge of the card, open up the card, and continue the line to a photocopied or hand-drawn map of your family's neighborhood or town (show your house or the reunion party site

as the end point for the line). Write the reunion details on the bottom of the invitation.

- Collect baby pictures from some of your older relatives, and photocopy them for the front of the invitations with "Guess who?" as a caption. Reveal their identities at the reunion.

- Write some family trivia questions on your invitations to be answered at the reunion. Try to make the questions obscure— little-known facts will be the most surprising and fun.

- Ask all family members to bring along photos to share with the group (see the Decorations section in this chapter for more details).

Old Neighborhood Reunion

- Draw the old neighborhood, labeled with each family name, and use it for the front of your invitation.

- Depending on how far away your neighbors have moved from the old neighborhood, trace a map of the appropriate city, county, state, or region of the country. Label the homes where an old neighbor has moved with a yellow flag. Draw lines from the new homes, scattered all over the map, to the old neighborhood. Use the map for the front of your invitation.

- Draw some mailboxes for the front of your invitation. On each mailbox, write the name of each of your former neighbors along with his or her *new* address. On the inside of the invitations, draw one large mailbox, and list all the names again.

- Photocopy old pictures of your guests to use for the front of your invitation, and write funny captions under each photo. Write the reunion information on the back.

- Send out a photocopy of a familiar neighborhood site with some special memories written around the photo. Fold it up, and write the reunion details inside.

School Reunion

- Photocopy a picture of your old high school, and place it on the front of the invitation with the school name and the years your class attended, such as "George Washington High School, 1961–1965." Then photocopy a picture of an old shack, write "George Washington High School, after 1965," and place it on the inside of the invitation along with the reunion information.

- Begin your invitation with trivia questions such as, "Who was voted class clown?" "Who was suspended for stealing the school mascot?" or "Who was the Prom Queen?" to jog everyone's memory and get people in the mood.

- Send out invitations in the school colors, with the school mascot on the front and the reunion information on the back.

- Pick out several funny pictures from the yearbook, and photocopy them for the front of the invitations with the caption "Where are they now?" displayed underneath. Borrow recent pictures of the same people, photocopy them, and mount them on the inside of the invitations with funny captions written underneath, such as "Head cheerleader at Herman's Automotive School" or "Serving five to ten for not getting a haircut." Write the reunion information on the back of the invitation.

- Contact some teachers from your old high school, and borrow recent photos of them. Mount photocopies of the pictures on the front of your invitation with funny captions written underneath (such as phrases they typically used in class). Write the reunion information on the inside of the invitation.

- Obtain a recent edition of your old high school's newspaper, and replace the articles with your own creative copy. Cut and paste the materials until it looks like a real newspaper again, photocopy it, and send it to your guests with the reunion details included in the mock articles.

Decorations

If the reunion will be held outdoors, keep your decorations simple—just set a big, welcoming table with loads of food, and you won't need much else. An indoor gathering might require a bit more work. Here are some suggestions for decorative touches at both indoor buffets and outdoor picnics:

Family Reunion

- If you're having a sit-down dinner for the whole crew, set up tables covered with Americana print tablecloths (or any pattern that's reminiscent of your family's heritage).

- Put a special gift for each guest at his or her place setting. For example, select a nephew's favorite comic book, an aunt's favorite flower, or a grandmother's favorite tea. Or place a photograph of a family member at each place setting.

- If you've saved mementos from past get-togethers, place them around the house with notes describing the memory.

- Make a large family tree from construction paper, and hang it on the wall. Cut out colorful leaves, and write the names of all the family members on them. As your guests arrive, have them add their leaves to the tree.

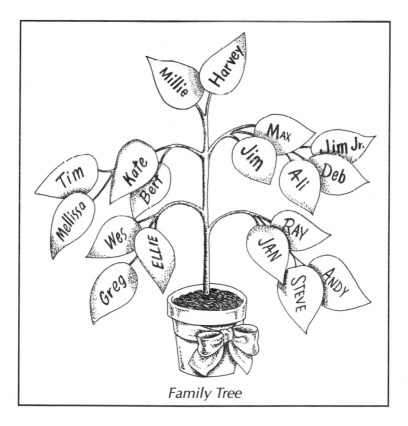

Family Tree

- Collect photographs of all family members, and place them around the house with descriptive captions underneath.

- Have T-shirts printed with the names (or signatures) of all the family members and the date of the family reunion. This makes a wonderful keepsake, and if you have several T-shirts printed at once, they won't be too expensive. If expense is a concern, you might request that your guests chip in some money to cover the cost.

- Ask all the family members to bring old family photo albums to share. Set them out on a special table for everyone to view during the reunion.

- Hang a large sheet of paper on the wall with the family name at the top written in fancy, colorful letters. Have each guest sign in by writing down a word of greeting or the description of a special event that has occurred during the year. Read the greetings aloud after everyone has arrived, or let people read them silently at their leisure.

- Assign one relative to greet guests and take them aside to either make silhouettes of their heads with black construction paper or full body outlines on large sheets of paper. Attach the designs to the walls as both decorations and lasting memories to share each year.

- Make name tags if you're expecting a big group. Give each family tags of a different color so long-lost relatives can tell the families apart.

Old Neighborhood Reunion

- If at all possible, hold your reunion somewhere in the old neighborhood. If no reunion members live there anymore, there might be a nearby park, favorite restaurant, or affordable hotel you can use instead.

- Tie large yellow ribbons around trees, posts, and mailboxes to welcome guests.

- Have your guests bring photos of their new homes to hang on the walls.

- Put photos of people from the old neighborhood all around the room.

- Decorate your party room to look like the old neighborhood. Cover large sheets of paper with drawings of old landmarks, houses, corner stores, and shops. Hang the large sheets on the walls to transform the room. Or if children are in attendance, have them use crayons to color the neighborhood scene—a great activity they'll have fun doing!

School Reunion

- Have T-shirts printed with all the names of your old class-mates.

- Enlarge some funny pictures from the old yearbook, and hang them on the walls.

- Decorate the party room in your school colors.

- Hang pennants made from construction paper that display the old school cheers or mottos.

- Hang "before" and "after" photos of the class officers, cheerleaders, sports figures, and other highly visible students by placing their graduation photos next to current ones.

- Re-create the senior prom with prom-theme wall hangings and appropriate music.

- Play songs popular during your teenage years.

- Create a "Where are they now?" wall presentation of funny things that have happened to former students over the years, using old photographs and funny captions. You can make up funny details or write down real events (which are often just as funny).

Games and Activities

At reunions, the adults usually spend much of their time catching up on news while the kids run off and play. But if you'd like to have a few organized activities, try some of the following. (Most of these are designed primarily for family reunions, but they can be adapted to suit most old neighborhood and school reunions as well.)

- Gather the group, and have family members state three things: (1) what they like best about their family, (2) a funny or unusual thing their family does, and (3) the best thing that ever happened to their family. This is a great way for long-lost relatives to get to know one another better.

- Ask family members to write down five of their worst dislikes on an index card. During the meal, read the cards one at a time, asking the group to guess which relative's dislikes you're reading. You can also have guests write down their likes, memories, fantasies, dreams, or anything else you think your group would enjoy hearing about.

- Ask each of your relatives beforehand to bring a quilt square, and join together at the reunion for a quilting bee. Assemble the squares while you talk over old times and catch up on family gossip. When the quilt finally comes together, hang it on the wall for everyone to share, and then bring it to each family gathering. If you make this a yearly tradition, choose a new theme each year, and allow different family members to keep the quilts until the next reunion. These quilts make lasting family heirlooms.

- Ask each family to bring a family photo to the reunion, and then place them all in an album. Bring the albums to other family gatherings to share.

- Make a videotape of each family member describing how he or she is related to the family.

- Ask each family member to bring along a family memory, and then share them one at a time during the gathering.

- Start a new tradition by having an "Elder's Story." To do this, ask the oldest family member to tell (or write and read aloud) the story of his or her life. This is a great way for younger family members to learn about their elders and their family history.

- Ask each family to bring a song to share, and then put together a complete family songbook. Have a sing-along or a "reunion band" concert!

- If many of the reunion guests at your party are unacquainted, play a variation of "Get-Acquainted Bingo" (see the Christmas Party chapter on p. 135 for more details). It's a great way to get everyone to mingle and catch up on the latest news.

- Collect little-known facts about each reunion member before the reunion (or do it discreetly during the reunion), and write the facts down beside the appropriate names. During activity time, gather your guests and read off each little-known fact. Ask everyone to try to guess who it relates to.

- Collect bits of family, neighborhood, or school trivia, and make up colorful trivia-question cards. For example, if you learned that a reunion member won $20 in the lottery, turn that into a question such as, "Who won $20 in the lottery last week?" Tape the question cards around the party room, and have everyone read and answer them. When everyone has had a chance to guess, read the questions aloud, and have the person who the question is about reveal the correct answer.

- Have an awards ceremony after the meal, with prizes or small trophies for the reunion member who traveled the farthest, ate the most, arrived the latest, made the best dessert, drove in the biggest car, and any other fun "milestones" you can think of.

- Have one or two adults take turns organizing and supervising games for any kids who are attending the reunion—try baseball, kickball, soccer, kick the can, badminton, kite flying, and "kitchen table" crafts.

- Show home movies after a busy day of socializing. Call all the guests ahead of time, and ask them to bring home movies, home videos, or slides. This is a great way for every-one to wind down and to catch up on old news.

Refreshments

If you're hosting a large gathering, the best refreshment idea is a potluck buffet—it's fun, and easy to prepare and clean up. Make a list of food categories that include the following:

- Appetizers: snacks, chips and dips, finger foods, raw vegetables, and fruits.

- Salads: green, gelatin, potato, macaroni, pasta, and fruit.

- Main dishes: meat, casseroles, tacos, pizza, sandwiches, quiche, and pasta.
- Breads: rolls, French bread loaves, muffins, biscuits, and crackers.
- Fruits and vegetables: hot, cold, cooked, raw, and casserole-style.
- Desserts: cakes, pies, cookies, brownies, ice cream, and fruit.
- Beverages: soda, beer, wine, milk, juice, punch, and water.

Ask each guest to bring a favorite dish from an assigned category, and check to see that you have all food categories covered. As the food arrives, label each dish with the name of the food and the cook's name, and refrigerate anything that might spoil. Serve all dishes buffet style with sturdy paper plates and cups and plastic utensils for each guest. Or, with family or old neighborhood gatherings, family members can be asked to bring their own dinnerware. Here are a few more suggestions for feeding the masses easily:

- Order a long poorboy sandwich (up to six feet) from a deli. The cost is reasonable, and the giant loaf makes an attractive conversation piece. Serve it with a serrated bread knife so guests can cut away lengths of the sandwich at their leisure.
- Have a pasta feast. To do this, a few days before the event, cook large pots full of various Italian sauces (marinara, clam, Alfredo, and pesto, to name a few), or ask some guests to bring a favorite pasta sauce. At mealtime, cook up four large pots full of four different pastas (spaghetti, fettucine, corkscrew, tortellini, or any favorite). Let your guests mix and match pastas and sauces. Serve with loaves of fresh French bread and a large green salad.
- Cook up a big pot of chili, and serve it with corn bread and a green salad. Offer sliced watermelon for dessert.
- Have a do-it-yourself shish kebab cook-out. To do this, cut steak or chicken into cubes, place it in bowls, and marinate it overnight. Cut up green pepper, onion, cherry tomatoes, mushrooms, corn-on-the-cob, zucchini, and pineapple, and place them in individual bowls. Give each guest a skewer, and let them create and cook their own shish kebab. Serve with rice and salad.

- Serve taco shells and fixings, and let everyone fill them to their liking.
- Ask each guest to bring a boxed lunch in a decorated shoe box, basket, or bandanna. Place all the boxed lunches on a big table, and draw numbers or hold a bid on the different boxes, without revealing the contents. If you auction the lunches off, use the money for games, prizes, or other shared expenses. If the boxes are decorated, award a prize for the most beautiful, funny, creative, and other categories.
- Serve a stunning and unique "patchwork cake" for dessert. On your reunion invitation, ask each guest to bring a piece of cake, 8 inches square, decorated with the name of the contributors on top. As guests arrive, take their cake squares, and place them side-by-side on a large table to form an enormous patchwork cake. The cake makes a wonderful centerpiece—don't forget to take a picture of it before it's all gone!

Patchwork Cake

- Have each guest bring a favorite dish to the reunion, along with photocopies of the recipe. Pass out the recipes (in the form of a cookbook, if you wish) to each reunion member.

Prizes and Gifts

The greatest satisfaction for your guests is the chance to see old friends again and make new acquaintances. But it's a good idea to provide some kind of party memento as a special reminder:

Prizes

- Coupon for a family portrait.
- Blank videotapes for making home videos.
- Inexpensive camera for taking family photos.
- Weekend vacation in a hotel for the whole family.
- Awards for the following categories: "Traveled the farthest," "Changed the most," "Forgot the most names," "Looks the youngest," and others that are appropriate for your reunion guests.

Gifts

- Have a T-shirt printed with the names or signatures of all the reunion members on it—a lasting keepsake!
- Have a group picture taken. You can send out copies to all the participants after your party is over. At the next reunion, you can enlarge the picture and use it as a decoration.
- Make a photocopy of the family tree.
- Have bumper stickers or pins made up with some special slogan from your group such as, "I'm a member of the Whozits family," "Smokerise Court—a chip off the old block," or "I Survived the Class of '65."
- Provide all of the guests with address books, and have everyone exchange addresses before they leave the party.
- Give stationery so everyone stays in touch.

Chapter 11

The Christmas season is a popular time for hosting a party—from the traditional Christmas Eve tree-trimming event for family members only to large open-house celebrations with lots of friends, food, and festivities. Here are some suggestions for celebrating this cheery time of year:

- Keep your party quiet and simple—just have friends over for a candlelight dinner and gift exchange.

- Invite your relatives to spend Christmas Eve caroling in front of the tree, around the neighborhood, or at a local convalescent center. End the evening with warm snacks and hot cider.

- Hold a get-together before or after church services, with a shared buffet dinner and special gift-opening ceremony.

- Host an open house during the holiday season, and invite old and new friends to share cocktails and appetizers, and the comforts of home.

- Have friends and neighbors over for a Christmas cocktail party, featuring a special theme or tradition.

- Gather your friends together for a gift-making party—an

informal get-together to share ideas and materials, work and talk, and eat and drink.

- Invite friends over for a "cookie exchange." To do this, ask your guests to bring three dozen homemade holiday cookies. For the cookie exchange, have everyone circle around the cookie table and collect three dozen assorted cookies to take home. This is a fun way to share Christmas joy without going to a lot of trouble, and the cookie table makes a festive display during your party. Be sure to have a few dozen cookies to nibble on during the exchange!

- Host an "ornament exchange." Ask your guests to bring a tree ornament, nicely wrapped but without a gift tag. During the party, gather your guests around the tree, and have them draw numbers to determine who goes first: the first guest selects the first wrapped ornament, followed by the second guest, the third, and so on until all the gifts are chosen. Then, have each guest unwrap the gift for all to see, and take it home to add to his or her own collection of ornaments.

  A variation on this ornament exchange is to have the first guest open a gift, and then let the second guest have the option of selecting a wrapped gift to open or taking the opened ornament from the first guest. This game continues, with the last guest having the fun of choosing anyone else's ornament or picking the last wrapped gift. No one is safe until the last ornament is opened, which adds considerable suspense.

Invitations
●●●●●●●●●●●●●●●

There are many fun and creative ways to invite guests to your Christmas party. Here are a few suggestions:

- Make your invitations out of cookie dough: Cut sugar cookie dough into circles, poke a small hole at the top to run string through, bake, and decorate with tubes of frosting. Write your party details on the cookie with a writing-tip tube of frosting (be patient!), and allow the frosting to dry. Run red string through the hole to make the cookie look like an ornament, and lay the cookie on tissue paper in a small box. Wrap the invitation up with Christmas gift wrap and hand-deliver.

- Write your party details on a white card with red and green ink for a festive touch, drop it in a flat box, and wrap the box with Christmas gift wrap.
- Buy 6-inch candy canes, and twist a brown or white pipe cleaner around the top of each one to form reindeer antlers. Glue plastic eyes (available at hobby or craft stores) on the candy canes. Tie a card with your party details written on it to each candy cane and hand-deliver.

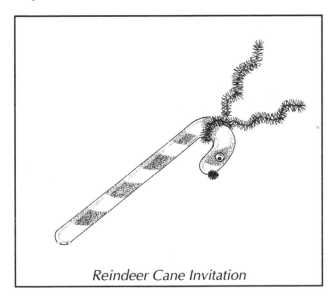

Reindeer Cane Invitation

- Cut out wreaths, ornaments, stars, or other Christmas symbols from construction paper, and write your party details on the back.
- Send a white card with your party information written in silver or gold ink, and place it in an envelope. Add several icicles made from aluminum foil to the envelope.
- Create a card featuring Santa's hat and hands peeking over the edge of a chimney. On the inside of the card, ask guests to "drop in for an open house."
- Make gingerbread men, each one decorated with a guest's

name on the front. Tie a card containing your party details to their feet and hand-deliver.

- Make baker's clay from 4 cups flour, 1 cup salt, and 1¾ cups water. Mix the ingredients together, add several drops of red or green food coloring, and knead the "clay" well. Roll out the dough, and use cookie cutters to cut it into stars, reindeer heads, or other Christmas shapes. Poke holes at the top for string, and bake on aluminum foil at 250° for two hours or until the clay is hard when touched with a fork. Allow ample cooling time; then write your party details on the back of each one with a felt-tip pen.

- Cut tagboard into star shapes, cover with foil, and write your party details on the top.

- Buy small poinsettia plants, and tie a card containing your party details to each one. Hand-deliver to your guests. (Cover the plants with plastic bags if the temperature is cold outside!)

- Write your party details on a white card, tie thin red and green ribbon around the interior fold, and attach a small bell to the ribbon.

- Buy 8-inch candy canes and brown felt. Cut out reindeer heads from the felt and glue other craft materials to form the heads. Glue on plastic eyes and a red pom-pom for the nose. Write your party details on a small card and hand-deliver.

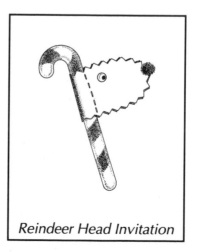

Reindeer Head Invitation

130

- Write your party details on a card in red and green ink. Tie a piece of ribbon around a sprig of mistletoe, and attach it to the card.

- Cut out ornaments from felt, and decorate them with liquid embroidery (available at fabric stores). Write your party details on the back with a felt-tip pen.

- Cut out berries and holly leaves from red and green felt or construction paper, and write your party details on the back.

- Photocopy or write down a favorite Christmas poem for the front of the invitation, and write your party details on the back.

- Photocopy or draw a favorite Christmas scene from a holiday book or greeting card for the front of the invitation, and write your party details on the back.

- Cut out a wreath from green felt. Glue tiny red felt circles around the wreath for berries, tie a thin red ribbon at the top of the wreath, and mount it on tagboard. Write your party details around the wreath.

- Purchase small, inexpensive ornaments, and attach them to a card containing your party details. Hand-deliver, or mail them in a small padded envelope or box.

Decorations
●●●●●●●●●●●●●●●●●

The decorations for your Christmas party should be easy—just unpack the box in the attic marked "Christmas," and transform your home into Santa's workshop. In addition to traditional decorations, strings of lights, glowing candles, and lots of Christmas music, here are some ideas to consider for getting your home, office, or party room ready for a holiday celebration:

- Use red and green felt to cover your tabletops, mantels, desks, and counters (it's easier to use than fabric because there's no hemming needed). You can also use felt for place mats, coasters, and a Christmas tree skirt.

- Hang fresh boughs of pine on the mantel and front door, and along bathroom counters.

- Place candy canes all around the house or party site.
- String your own cranberry or popcorn garlands, and hang them on the tree, drape them on the mantel, set them on window ledges, or use them to frame your table setting.
- Tie sprigs of mistletoe with red and green ribbon, and hang them in doorways, in the kitchen, and over the toilet for a laugh.
- Buy some small poinsettia plants, and place them on the fireplace, on either side of the front door, on tables, in clusters on the floor, or on the mantel. (If you have small children or pets, keep the poinsettias out of reach as they can be mildly toxic if ingested.)
- Tape or pin small, colorful Christmas stockings, Santas, candy canes, and ornaments to doors throughout the house or party area. Or think of some creative places to hang them to surprise your guests.
- Buy bags of polyester fiberfill or angel hair, and drape the material over tables and shelves for an "indoor blizzard." Then set your decorations and food on top.
- Buy a roll of colored foil gift wrap, and tape or staple it securely to two large sheets of tagboard that, when fit together, are the size of your front door. Buy bags of sourballs, Hershey's kisses, and other wrapped candies, and glue (or tape) them to the paper. Allow the glue to dry, and then tape the tagboard sections to the door to make a brilliant and exciting welcome for your guests. Or "wrap" your front door with colored foil gift wrap, and "tie" a big red bow to it—your door will look like a giant present!
- Make garlands for your Christmas tree and mantel from wrapped hard candies. To do this, buy a variety of candies, and tie their twisted ends to the ends of other candies with red and green curling ribbon. Repeat this until you have the length of garland you want, and then curl the ends of the ribbon with scissors.
- Make a "gingerbread" house with a square cardboard box. Use an extra sheet of cardboard, folded in half, to form a roof, and tape the roof section to the square box. Cover the box with

colored foil gift wrap, and glue cellophane- and foil-wrapped candies to it, in patterns, until the entire surface is covered. Set it on polyester fiberfill or angel hair so it looks as if it's surrounded by snow.

- Make a teddy bear ornament tree. To do this, buy a small Christmas tree and set it up on a table. Make baker's clay teddy bears for all your guests. Stick paper clips into the tops of their heads to form hooks before baking. After baking and cooling, paint them with brown acrylic paint, adding facial details with black paint. Hang them, by their hooks, to the tree. (These cute ornaments can be given out at the end of your party as gifts, prizes, or favors.)

Teddy Bear Ornament

- Make large candy-cane reindeer (see the Invitations section in this chapter for details), and set them in a tall canister or bowl so that their faces are peeking over the edge. Fill the canister or bowl with other goodies, such as holiday M&Ms or hard candies. Give the reindeer to your guests to take home at the end of the party.
- Dress up as Santa, Mrs. Claus, or an elf. Wear bells, or attach

bells to all your guests as they walk in the door.

- Make up a batch of sugar cookies and roll to ½-inch thick. With a sharp knife, cut out letters to spell a holiday greeting— "Merry Christmas," "Joy to the World," or "Bah, Humbug!" Bake the cookies according to package or recipe directions, and let them cool. Outline your holiday greeting with a decorator tube of red or green frosting (available at confectionery or bakery supply stores). Add a tiny holly leaf and little berries to the corners of the letters, and lay them out on tables or prop them up along windowsills or the mantel.

- Hang Santa's legs in your fireplace (if you're not having a fire!) so it looks as if he's coming down the chimney. To do this, cut out his legs and boots from felt and his boot tops from felt or fiberfill. Hang them in the fireplace for a whimsical effect.

Santa Fireplace Decoration

- Dress your table with an inexpensive Christmas pattern from a fabric store. Buy two table lengths worth of pattern, cut them in half, and sew them together along the sides to form tablecloths.

- Make elf hats from red and green felt for all your guests. Attach a pom-pom to the top, along with a small bell, and dress your guests as elves when they enter the party room.

- Decorate your windows with spray "frost" or "snow," using a lace doily for a stencil (decorative sprays are available at holiday time in most drug or party goods supply stores, along with holiday stencils), or cut out snowflakes from white paper and tape them to the windows.

- Make a "stained-glass" window by designing a Christmas picture, outlining the design with black felt or construction paper on your chosen window, and filling in the spaces with colored cellophane.

Games and Activities

Christmas parties usually don't require much in the way of games or activities—most of your guests will simply enjoy meeting new people, seeing old friends, and sharing good cheer.

Unfortunately, some people don't mix well, are timid about meeting new friends, and are shy about introducing themselves to strangers. Here are several games to help people get acquainted, and to put them in the holiday spirit:

- Get-Acquainted Bingo: Although this game might take some time in preparation, it helps strangers get acquainted and encourages mingling later on.

  First, cut green and red construction paper into 3-by-4-inch cards—one for each guest. With a pencil, draw a grid dividing each card into six equal squares. Write the name of one guest on the top middle square on the front of each card. Write a question in each of the five remaining squares pertaining to various guests, such as "Who just had a baby?" "Who was promoted to lieutenant of the police force last week?" "Who just returned from a two-month vacation in Germany?" or "Who here is an award-winning gourmet cook?" You can use the same questions on several cards, but be sure to have a question about each guest.

  Cut out and place five Christmas stickers on the back of each card—keep the stickers on their original paper backings and glue or tape them to the card backs. When your guests arrive, give them their "Get-Acquainted Bingo" cards, and tell them they will receive a prize if they are able to fill up their cards by locating the five people connected with the five questions. They are to approach other guests and ask the questions on their card. If they find someone to match the question on the card, they are to take a sticker from that person and place it over the answered question. When your guests fill all five spaces on their cards with stickers, award them a small prize, such as a teddy bear ornament or a candy cane reindeer (see the Decorations section in this chapter).

- Match Game: Find two objects that go together—salt and pepper shakers, a spoon and fork, needle and thread, and so on—and collect enough pairs for all your guests. You might want to make the pairs more obscure for added fun, such as two computer items, two musical items, or two gardening items, so people have to think a little more about which things go together. Write the names of your guests on small, sticky labels and attach one name to each item, being sure to match strangers when possible. Then distribute the objects around your party room by taping them in plain sight to tables, walls, lamps, and chairs. During the evening, have your guests locate their names and objects and find their partners. At dinner, partners should be seated together.

- Christmas Trivia: Write questions related to Christmas on little green Christmas tree cutouts, number them, and tape them to the walls around the party room. Provide your guests with pencil and paper, and have them write down their answers to the numbered questions. Here are some of the questions to get you started:

  1. What is a bûche de Nöel? (an edible yule log)
  2. What do bad little boys get for Christmas? (switches and lumps of coal)
  3. Finish the song line: "All I want for Christmas is . . ." (my two front teeth)
  4. Who was caught kissing Santa Claus? (Mommy)
  5. How do you say Merry Christmas in Spanish and French? (Feliz Navidad, Joyeux Nöel)
  6. What are the names of Santa's eight reindeer? (Dasher, Dancer, Prancer, Vixen, Comet, Cupid, Donner, and

Blitzen)

7. What did Frosty the Snowman have for a nose? (a carrot)

8. Who wrote "The Night Before Christmas?" (Clement Clarke Moore)

9. What is the last line in "The Night Before Christmas?" (Happy Christmas to all, and to all a good night.)

10. What is a "Tannenbaum?" ("Christmas tree," in German)

11. What did the Three Wise Men bring? (gold, frankincense, and myrrh)

12. On the twelfth day of Christmas, what did "my true love give to me"? (twelve fiddlers fiddling, eleven lords a-leaping, ten ladies dancing, nine pipers piping, eight maids a-milking, seven swans a-swimming, six geese a-laying, five golden rings, four calling birds, three French hens, two turtle doves, and a partridge in a pear tree)

13. Which two reindeer on Santa's team have German names that mean "thunder" and "lightning"? (Donner and Blitzen)

Here are some additional get-acquainted game ideas for your party:

- Buy a collection of candy canes, and break them in half. Give the bent halves to your male guests and the straight halves to your female guests as they enter your party, and have everyone find their match.

- Make sugar cookies in the shape of round ornaments. Cut the circles in half, using a jagged line or puzzle-like cut, and separate the halves slightly. Bake the cookies according to package or recipe directions. When cool, decorate them like ornaments. As your guests arrive, give them a cookie half and have them find their "other half."

- Play a version of "Facts" (see the Reunions chapter on p. 123 for more details), tailoring it to your group of guests.

- Have a Christmas scavenger hunt. To do this, divide your guests into teams or couples, and give them a list of Christmas-related items to locate, either in the house or around the neighborhood. List items such as a candle, a religious Christmas card, some mistletoe, a Christmas cookie, a broken ornament, a burned-out tree light, a Christmas stamp, some tinsel, and a few pine needles.

- Ask your guests to bring an inexpensive, wrapped gift (appropriate for either a man or woman), with no gift tag on it. Have your guests draw numbers and choose their gifts in numerical order (or have your guests pick them out blindfolded). Allow everyone to make a trade if they wish.

- Have a "cookie exchange" or "ornament exchange" (see the Invitations section in this chapter).

- Hire Santa to make a surprise visit and hand out gifts.

Refreshments

Nothing welcomes guests better than a party room filled with the enticing aromas of Christmas. Bake your own specialties, and add a few of these quick-and-easy holiday treats:

Drinks

- Have a large pot of hot mulled wine simmering on the stove. Heat red wine with several sticks of cinnamon, some cloves, and a little nutmeg, or stick cloves all over small apples or oranges (oranges are preferred!), and let them float in the wine. Serve this to your guests as they arrive.

- Prepare a pot of hot apple cider mixed with cranberry juice cocktail for a nonalcoholic beverage.

- If you're offering champagne, place a small peppermint stick inside each glass. (Here's another tip: Many guests set their drinks down and forget where they put them. As each guest arrives, write his or her initials on a small peel-and-stick circle, and stick it onto the top or base of the glass. That way guests can check to see which glass belongs to them).

- Offer cinnamon coffee as a finale. Serve mugs of coffee with a stick of cinnamon and a dollop of whipped cream on top.

Desserts

- Serve "sherbet ornaments": With an ice cream scooper, scoop balls of raspberry, orange, and lime sherbet (and other fla-vors, if desired) onto a platter and store in the freezer until serving time. At the party, set the platter out with small plates or bowls.

- Try do-it-yourself peppermint sundaes featuring peppermint ice cream and bowls full of toppings such as nuts, crushed candy canes, mini chocolate chips, crushed Oreo cookies, coconut, chocolate sauce, and fresh mint.

- Create petits fours "presents": Start by baking a large white sheet cake. When it's done baking (and still hot), poke holes in the cake and cover the top with an orange juice glaze made from ¼ cup orange juice and 2 tablespoons powdered sugar mixed together. Allow the cake to cool, then cut it into small squares. Make frosting, and dilute with a little water so it will pour. Pour the frosting over small cakes, and allow it to dry. Decorate with a fine-tip frosting tube to make each cake look like a "present" by crossing two lines and adding a star, bow, or flower in the center.

- Serve your guests champagne "snowballs." Mix 2 cups lemon sherbet, ½ cup champagne, and 4 ice cubes in a blender. Serve the mixture in champagne glasses with a lemon twist.

- Make a simple yule log by baking a chocolate cake on a cookie sheet or jelly roll pan, icing it with white buttercream frosting, and rolling it up into a log. Frost it with chocolate frosting (swirling the frosting for a "bark" effect), and top it with cherry halves and chopped walnuts.

Appetizers

- Make an appetizer tree. Buy a large Styrofoam cone at a hobby or crafts store and cover it with fancy lettuce leaves—endive and watercress, preferably. Prepare lots of bite-size vegetables and fruits, skewer them with toothpicks, and poke them into the "tree." Present it with a dressing or dip.

- Serve cheese, bread, and deli meats cut into Christmas shapes with small cookie cutters.

- Make a red and green platter of crudités with cherry tomatoes, red and green peppers, celery, lightly steamed pea pods, and red cabbage. Healthy food for the holiday!

Prizes, Gifts, and Favors

Christmas parties should be filled with special holiday mementos. Try some of these thoughtful presents, wrapped in festive paper and tied with red and green curling ribbon:

Prizes

- Box of candy canes or chocolate-covered cherries.
- Book of Christmas stories.
- Tape or CD of Christmas music by a popular singer or group.
- Christmas ornament or decoration.

Gifts

Try to personalize your gifts, if you know who they're going to, and add some humor if you like. The following are good examples:

- For your friend, the cosmetics salesperson, offer a bottle of cologne from a competitor.
- For your guest who just returned from the tropics, offer an hour in a tanning booth.
- For your co-worker with a new car, offer a funny bumper sticker such as, "My Other Car Is a Hunk of Junk."

Or give gifts appropriate for all ages:

- Box of candy.
- Board game.
- Humor book.
- Funny holiday socks.
- Videotape of *It's a Wonderful Life*.
- Jar of jelly beans or homemade jam.

Favors

- Santa hats.
- Homemade fudge on holiday paper plates.
- Fruitcake.
- Loaf of holiday bread.
- Candy canes decorated like reindeer (see directions on pp. 129–30).
- Oranges covered with clove spikes and tied with ribbon for hanging—makes a fragrant pomander!
- Inexpensive Christmas tree ornaments.

Chapter 12

In December, the Feast of Lights is celebrated during an eight-day period. This is a time when you and your family, neighbors, and co-workers will celebrate with special parties, home get-togethers with gift-exchanges and games, and worship at the local synagogue. Light a candle on the menorah for each day of Hanukkah, and celebrate the rich traditions of the Jewish heritage. Here are some traditional and modern ways to help you observe this wonderful holiday.

Invitations

Try these invitation ideas for inviting friends and relatives to your Hanukkah party:

- Draw a nine-branched menorah on gold or yellow construction paper, and cut it out. You might want to represent light-ed candles by cutting out "flames" from yellow or orange construction paper and gluing them to the menorah. Write your party details on the back.

- Make six-pointed Star of David invitations by cutting out triangles from white and blue construction paper. Hollow-out the two triangles by cutting out another large triangle from the middle of both. To make the Star look authentic, cut through one triangle and weave the blue and the white triangles as shown in the illustration. Glue them together. Write your party details on the edges of the triangles.

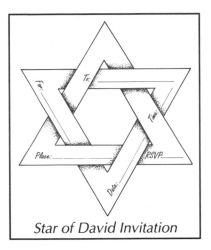

Star of David Invitation

- Write your party details on a small white card in blue ink. Attach the card to a small white candle with string or glue and hand-deliver.
- Cut out a small hammer from construction paper to use as a symbol of the patriot Maccabaeus. Write your party details on the back.

Decorations

Keep the decorations for your Hanukkah party simple and traditional. Consider some of the following ideas:

- Set a menorah (with the appropriate number of candles lit) in a front window to welcome your guests. Cut out menorahs from construction paper to hang on the walls.
- Cut out six-pointed stars from construction paper, and hang

144

them on the walls or dangle them from the ceiling.

- Decorate the party room in traditional Jewish colors—blue and white. Party goods supply stores should carry blue and white crepe paper, paper plates and cups, and other decorations.

- Write down some Hebrew phrases and hang them on the walls, such as "Nes Gadol Hayah Sham" which means "A great miracle happened there" or "Shalom" which is a greeting meaning "peace."

- Play traditional Hebrew music, such as "Ma'oz Tzur."

Games and Activities

Celebrate Hanukkah with the following party suggestions:

- The most popular game during Hanukkah is a game of chance—the spinning of the dreidel. Each Hebrew letter on the four-sided top/dreidel stands for a game action:

    N (*nun*)   = Get nothing from the kitty.
    G (*gimel*)   = Get everything from the kitty.
    H (*he*)   = Get half of the kitty.
    S (*shin*)   = Put half the money in the kitty.

Dreidel

If you don't have a dreidel already, you can purchase one at a party goods supply or toy store (they're also fun to make at home from craft materials). Have your guests bring pennies, gold-foil-wrapped chocolate coins, or candies to put in the kitty, or distribute these items yourself during game time. Have everyone place a penny or candy into the kitty, and then take turns spinning the dreidel to determine who wins and who loses. At the end of the game, have everyone count their winnings, and use the pennies and candies to purchase small, wrapped gifts that you've prepared ahead of time.

- Card games are traditional activities during Hanukkah. Learn a few new games, or play old favorites like Canasta, Gin, Hearts, and Bridge.

Refreshments

Serve traditional food items like potato latkes and milk dishes, or prepare variations to traditional recipes to suit your own taste and style. Here are some delicious recipes to try:

- Potato latkes: Peel 2 pounds of russet potatoes, and place them in a large pan full of water and 1 tablespoon lemon juice. Coarsely shred the potatoes directly into the lemon-water mixture, and keep them submerged. Beat 1 egg with 2 tablespoons flour, 1/3 cup finely chopped onion, 1 teaspoon salt, a dash of pepper, and 1/2 teaspoon caraway seeds. Drain the potatoes, squeezing out as much moisture as possible. Add the potatoes to the egg mixture and stir well. Melt 4 tablespoons margarine in a frying pan and heat to medium. Spoon 1/2 cup potato mixture into the frying pan, gently spreading it into a 4-inch circle. Cook two or three latkes at a time, turning each one once, until they're crisp and golden brown on both sides. Arrange the potato pancakes on a baking sheet, and warm them in the oven at 200° until the rest of the latkes are cooked. Serves eight.

- Quiche: Buy or make a pie crust, and prick it all over with a fork. Bake for 5 minutes in a preheated oven at 375°. Sauté 1/2 cup chopped onion in 1 tablespoon margarine. Sprinkle 1/2 pound grated Swiss cheese over the bottom of the pie crust.

Top with the sautéed onion. Beat 3 eggs, and then add 1 1/4 cups light cream, 1/2 teaspoon salt, 1/4 teaspoon pepper, 1/2 teaspoon dry mustard, and 1/4 teaspoon nutmeg—beat the mixture together. Pour the mixture into the pie crust, and bake at 375° for 40 minutes until the center is set. Let it stand 10 minutes, then cut it into wedges or small squares. Serves eight. Optional ingredients: sautéed mushrooms, cooked spinach, or meat and vegetables of your choice.

Prizes, Gifts, and Favors

Memorable Hanukkah gifts and keepsakes will delight your party guests. Here are a few suggestions:

- Dreidels.
- Gold-foil-wrapped chocolate coins to symbolize gifts of money or "gelt."
- New coins set in key rings or paperweights.
- Recipes for traditional Jewish dishes (you could even have a recipe exchange) or Jewish cookbooks.
- Candles or menorahs.
- Blue and white items, such as ceramic dishware, socks, or stationery.

Chapter 13

If it's time to celebrate the birth of a new year, you can host a traditional late-night New Year's Eve party or opt for an afternoon of football and food at your New Year's Day party. Here are some fun party ideas to consider:

- If you're planning to have a New Year's Eve party, you might want to begin on the late side of the evening—8:00 or 9:00 P.M.—since it's almost guaranteed to run into the wee hours. If you're serving alcohol, be sure to give your guests plenty of snacks or provide a late-night supper—drinking on an empty stomach is dangerous, and you want your guests to get home safely when the party is over. Make sure guests leaving your party are sober enough to drive, take a cab, or ride with a designated driver. Any "Best Party" host will take extra precautions when it comes to drinking and driving!

- Try serving a buffet breakfast right after midnight—after all, it's morning! This is a nice way to begin the New Year (unless your resolution is to diet) and a good way to sober up your guests.

- Dress up your party by having a "black-and-white ball": Ask your guests to wear only black and white, but to be creative in the way they do it—you might end up with one guest in a tuxedo, one in a black and white bathing suit, another in some black and white exercise wear, and yet another in a black leather jacket and white shorts. Make your party's color scheme match the black and white theme.

- Have a regal costume ball, with outlandish getups and flamboyant masks. Award prizes for a variety of costume categories, or vote on the most creative homemade mask.

- Since it's the beginning of another year, have your guests come seasonally dressed as per your specific instructions. Assign each person or couple a particular month, and ask them to dress appropriately. If it's a small group, just assign them to dress as one of the four seasons.

- Have a "Highlights of 19XX" party. Ask each guest to come dressed in an outfit that represents a major or minor event that took place during the year. Half the fun is guessing what event each guest represents!

- Host a pajama party: Have your guests wear pajamas for your evening of celebration, and ask them to bring along sleeping bags if you don't have accommodations for everyone. (This way no one has to drive home.) Have a pillow fight, or ask your guests to model their outfits for the crowd while you give a "fashion commentary." In the morning, serve a simple breakfast of pastries, juice, and coffee to perk everyone up.

- If you're having the gang over for New Year's Day, focus on football and food. Serve a buffet brunch or potluck lunch, and decorate with your team's colors. Then sit back and enjoy the game.

Invitations

Begin your New Year's celebration with some festive invitations:

- Write your party details on a white card, and fill the envelope with colorful confetti. You can make confetti by cutting up colored paper, or you can buy it at a party goods supply store.

- Write your party details on a party hat or horn, and slip the invitation into a large envelope.

- Buy plastic champagne glasses, and write your party details on them with a felt-tip pen. Tie colorful curling ribbon to the stems of the glasses, and curl the ends. Hand-deliver or mail in a box.

Champagne Glass Invitation

- Tear off the page containing the date of your party (December 31st or January 1st) from a wall or desk calendar, and write your party details on it. Photocopy it for all your guests.

- Write your party information on streamers, and place the streamers in an envelope.

- Make small clocks from white tagboard, cut out clock hands from black tagboard, and attach the hands to the clock face with a fastener. Write your party details on the clock.

- Create your own end-of-the-year newspaper. Use a typewriter or computer to write your party information in the form of a newspaper article. Cut and paste your party details on the current front page of your newspaper, change the date to December 31st or January 1st, and photocopy. Add a few headlines from the past year to embellish it, if you wish.

- Collect plastic champagne corks, and write your party details on them with a fine-tip pen. Or write the details on a card, and tie the card to the cork. Mail them out in a padded envelope.

- If you're having a "black-and-white ball," write your party details in black ink on a white card, and glue the white card onto a slightly larger black card. Punch a hole in one corner, and loop a strand of black and white ribbon through it. Mail it in a black or white envelope.

- If you're hosting a costume ball, write your party details on an inexpensive mask. You might also ask your guests to turn the mask into a wild false face and wear it to the ball. Tell them there will be a prize for the best one.

- For an "all-nighter," write your party details on cards tied to inexpensive toothbrushes, or make teddy bears from construction paper and send them out as invitations. You could also draw a moon on the cover of a card and a sun on the inside, as a background for your party information.

- If you're having a football party on New Year's Day, cut out footballs from brown construction paper. Or write your party details on construction paper in the favored team's colors. You might ask your guests to dress in their team's colors, too. For an hysterical and nostalgic trip back to high school, have your male guests wear old football jerseys and your female guests dress as cheerleaders (or vice versa!).

Decorations

Decorations for a New Year's celebration should be festive and full of color. Here are a few suggestions:

- Spread confetti and streamers over the tables in your party room. Hang thin paper streamers from the ceiling, and loop wider crepe paper streamers from the center of the ceiling to the walls.

- Make a large tagboard clock with black, movable hands. Or make lots of little clocks from white tagboard, one for each of your guests. Count down to midnight using the hands of the clock.

- Set your table with white paper plates. Draw a clock face on each plate with a black felt-tip pen, and cover with clear Contact paper.

- Fill deflated balloons with large spoonfuls of confetti by inserting a funnel into the mouth of each balloon and sliding the confetti inside. Take the balloons to a party goods supply store, and ask them to fill them up with helium, being careful not to spill the confetti. Tie the balloons with colorful ribbon streamers, and let them float up to the ceiling of your party room. At midnight, pull down a balloon, hold it over a friend's head, and pop it. . . . .

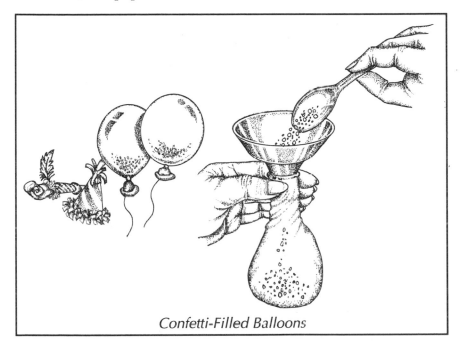

Confetti-Filled Balloons

- Decorate the walls of your party room with old newspaper headlines from the past year, or use old newspapers as place mats. Using decorative hand lettering or a computer, paste in a phony headline about each guest to mark his or her place.

- If you're hosting a "black-and-white ball," use black and white party accessories—a tablecloth, place mats, plates, and cups. Decorate with black and white balloons, streamers, and confetti.

- If you're having a costume party, borrow some costumes and props from a costume store, and use them for a centerpiece and decorations throughout the party room. You can usually rent terrific masks and other props for very little money—they really set the mood for a fun party.

- For an "all-nighter," hang stars and moons from the ceiling (you can cut them out from cardboard and cover them with aluminum foil), get out your spare teddy bears for a centerpiece, and play lullaby (or more lively!) music during the evening.

- If you're having a football party on New Year's Day, make pennants from construction paper for both teams, and tack them to the walls. Set your table with plates and cups in the favored team's colors, and buy accessories at a sporting goods store—miniature helmets, football cards, stickers, posters, and pennants.

- Make sure you have plenty of horns, hats, noisemakers, and confetti on hand!

Games and Activities

Here are a few game ideas to help you ring in the new year:

- Have your guests predict who the top ten men and women of the year are. At the end of every year, the newspapers and magazines (*People* and *Newsweek*, for example) list the top ten men and women of the year—save the list, and ask your guests to write down who they think won the awards. Reveal the answers, and award a prize to the guest who got the most correct.

- Pick out twelve major events that happened over the year— one from each month. (Check your library for old newspapers or magazines with the year in review.) Mix up the events, read them aloud one at a time, and ask your guests to write down the month in which each one took place.

  A variation on this game is to write down some of the more obscure holidays during the year—Groundhog Day, Mother-in-Law Day, National Secretary's Week, National Ice Cream

Day—and ask your guests to give the corresponding dates.

- Have everyone write predictions for each guest at your party. The predictions can be serious—"(Name) will get pregnant." or "(Name) will have a financial windfall."; or they can be ridiculous—"(Name) will win the lottery." or "(Name) will join a nunnery." Read the predictions aloud, and then save them to read again at your next New Year's Party.

A variation on this game is for the host to write the predictions, making them general with no names attached. Attach each prediction to a wrapped gift that corresponds to the prediction. For example, if you write, "You're going to have another child," attach it to a baby book or bottle. Tell your guests that some New Year's predictions are hidden around the room and that if they find one, they are to claim it, read the prediction, and open the gift. Each guest should claim only one gift.

New Year's Predictions

- Ask your guests to write three New Year's resolutions. Collect their answers, and then read each of them aloud, asking your guests to guess whose resolutions they are. This game will get everyone laughing!
- Ask your guests to come dressed as their favorite year, and then have everyone guess the year. Or have them dress as an

155

event that happened during the year.

- Write down some of the major events of the year, and ask two guests at a time to act out the scene for everyone to guess.

- Have a white elephant exchange: Ask each guest to select the worst, ugliest, or most useless present they received for Christmas or Hanukkah (if they didn't get anything really bad, they can bring something bizarre they've kept hidden away in a dark closet or attic). Ask them to wrap the "gifts" beautifully, bring them to your party, and set them on a display table. Have the oldest guest pick a gift from the table and unwrap it for all to admire. The next-oldest guest then has a choice—he or she can either select another wrapped gift or take away the gift that has just been unwrapped and have the preceding guest select another wrapped gift. Continue until all guests have opened a present.

- If you're hosting a "black-and-white ball," ask your guests to make a list of phrases that have to do with black or white, or both. For example, they might write: "We're finally in the black." "She turned white as a ghost." or "Nothing's black or white." Have the guest with the longest list read it aloud, and then have other guests read any that were missed. Award a black-and-white gift to the guest with the longest list.

- If you're hosting a football party on New Year's Day, make a football pool.

- End the evening with dancing to the year's favorite hits. Or have a "Name That Tune" game (using the year's biggest hits) by playing a portion of a song and having your guests race to name the title, artist, and perhaps even the month it was released.

Refreshments

Here are a few suggestions for some fancy, but easy-to-make, New Year's party refreshments:

- Serve champagne with a cherry at the bottom of each glass. Or make delicious strawberry or banana daiquiris, and serve them with a skewer of fruit slices.

- Serve a creme brulee—a rich, elegant dessert that's not difficult to make and requires few ingredients. In a large saucepan, heat 1 quart heavy cream until bubbles begin to form. *Do not boil.* Add 6 tablespoons sugar, and stir until dissolved. Beat 8 egg yolks until they're lemon-colored. Slowly add the hot cream to the eggs, stirring constantly until smooth. Add 2 teaspoons vanilla, blend, and pour into 8 custard cups. Place in a pan filled with 1 inch hot water, and bake for 35 minutes at 350°. Cool and chill for 4 hours. Sprinkle 1 cup brown sugar over the tops of the custards to ¼-inch thick and broil 3 minutes, until sugar has caramelized. Watch them carefully to avoid burning. Serve the custards well-chilled.

- Fill cream puffs with vanilla ice cream and thawed, packaged strawberries or chocolate mousse. Top with whipped cream and a cherry.

- If you're serving an after-midnight breakfast, mix up omelette batter and make individual omelettes for your guests. Prepare bowls of sliced mushrooms, bacon, ham, green onions, Cheddar cheese, Monterey Jack cheese, tomatoes, olives, or anything else you like in an omelette. Pour the omelette batter in a small frying pan, and add requested extras. Serve with a pour-on cheese sauce or salsa, and muffins. Or make your favorite popover recipe, adding ½ cup grated Cheddar cheese to the batter or ¼ cup cinnamon. Serve with honey, butter, or jam.

- Fix a hearty soup or casserole with black-eyed peas—the peas will give you good luck in the new year, according to an old custom popular in the Southern United States!

- For a "black-and-white ball," serve white chocolate mousse with dark chocolate shavings on top. Serve piña coladas and chocolate-flavored coffee.

- For a football party, order a long poor boy sandwich (up to six feet) from a deli, or make it a "day at the ballpark" with franks, sauerkraut, hot pretzels, roasted peanuts, and beer.

Prizes, Gifts, and Favors

Prizes

The new year always starts off well with good friends gathering together and a few special mementos:

- Book about astrology or predicting the future.
- Clock.
- Humorous calendar for the new year.
- Diet book.
- Bottle of champagne.
- Fancy coffee mug with a packet of coffee and two aspirin tablets inside.

Gifts

- Anything will work for a white elephant gift—the tackier the better. Surely you have something in your closet . . . .

Favors

- Bag of fortune cookies.
- Funny list of resolutions personalized for each guest.
- Quit-smoking (or other vice) manual.
- Bag of confetti, hat, and noisemaker.
- Packet of seeds to plant for the coming year.
- Alka Seltzer.
- The *Newsweek* "Year in Review," rolled up and tied with ribbon.
- Polaroid photos taken during the party.

HOLIDAY PARTIES

Chapter 14

If you're just looking for an excuse to have a party, nearly every month provides a major or minor holiday to celebrate. You might want to find a copy of *Chase's Annual Events* by William and Mary Chase (Contemporary Books, published annually). It contains a creative listing of a variety of special days, so you'll find hundreds of ideas for party themes. Here are some examples of honored days you might want to celebrate in the coming year:

January 9 - Sherlock Holmes's Birthday: Host a mystery party.

19 - Edgar Allen Poe's Birthday: Read works by Poe, put on a play of "The Raven," or rent horror movies adapted from Poe's tales.

26 - India National Holiday: Serve traditional Indian food and have your guests wear Indian garb.

27 - Mozart's Birthday: Attend a symphony or host a screening of *Amadeus*.

29 - Last Day of January, Chinese New Year:

Celebrate with Chinese food, kite-making, and costumes.

February 1 - Canned Food Month: Have everyone bring a can of soup to pour into the community soup pot for dinner.

7 - National Inventor's Day: Have your guests bring a silly invention they've created.

20 - First American in Space: Rent a "space" movie, such as *Aliens*, *Star Wars*, or *The Right Stuff*.

22 - International Friendship Week: Have a party where everyone brings one new friend.

28 - End of February, Carnival in Brazil: Host your own carnival with costumes and Brazilian food, music, and dancing.

March 2 - Texas Independence Day: Have a Texas-style barbecue and square dance.

6 - Michelangelo's Birthday: Visit an art museum with the gang.

20 - Earth Day: Do something for the planet (plant trees, pick up litter, recycle), and then party afterward.

24 - Harry Houdini's Birthday: Do magic tricks for your guests, or hire a magician.

25 - Pecan Day: Have everyone bring a dish that has pecans as an ingredient.

April 1 - April Fool's Day: Have a party, and play lots of practical jokes.

18 - Paul Revere's Ride: Take the gang horseback riding.

19 - Bike Safety Week: Organize a long-distance bike ride and picnic.

20 - Reading Is Fun Week: Start a monthly literary discussion group—read favorite novels, and

then share opinions and insights.

23 - William Shakespeare's Birthday: Put on a play for fun, or screen a movie adapted from the Bard's work; dress up in Elizabethan garb and serve turkey drumsticks and port wine.

May 1 - May Day: Have a picnic in a flower garden.

2 - Kentucky Derby: Go to the races.

11 - Bob Marley Day: Play lots of reggae music, dance all night, and serve Jamaican-inspired refreshments.

26 - John Wayne's Birthday: Watch a "Duke" movie, and ask everyone to wear their cowboy duds.

27 - Isadora Duncan's Birthday: Go dancing.

June 1 - National Safe Boating Week: Take a boat ride with your friends.

7 - Day of the Rice God: Have a rice potluck party, and share recipes.

11 - King Kamehameha Day: Have a Hawaiian luau with a roast pig and lots of pineapple.

20 - National Tennis Week: Host a tennis match.

24 - Flying Saucer Anniversary: Rent an old '50s "flying saucer" movie, such as *The Day the Earth Stood Still*, and eat popcorn.

July 6 - Caribbean Day: Go to the nearest beach or pool in your tropical shirts and muumuus.

12 - National Ice Cream Month: Host a make-your-own sundae affair.

14 - Bastille Day: Celebrate with French food, costumes, music, and wine.

22 - Croquet Commemoration Day: Have a croquet tournament.

30 - Henry Ford's Birthday: Take a short car trip

or caravan with friends, and then have a tailgate party.

August 1 - National Clown Week: Have your guests dress as clowns, serve circus food, and rent a Jerry Lewis movie.

6 - PGA Championship Golf: Go golfing or miniature golfing.

13 - Alfred Hitchcock's Birthday: Rent *The Birds*, *Vertigo*, and *Rear Window*, and have a Hitchcock marathon.

15 - National Relaxation Day: Have everyone sit around the pool or yard sipping cool drinks.

29 - "According to Hoyle" Day: Play all sorts of card games.

September 5 - Woodstock Fair: Play '60s music and wear tie-dyed clothes.

6 - National Frisbee Festival: Play Frisbee on the beach or at a park.

15 - Agatha Christie's Birthday: Go to a mystery play or rent an Agatha Christie movie, and try to figure out "who dunnit."

24 - Rosh Hashanah: Celebrate the Jewish New Year with traditional Jewish dishes.

26 - Johnny Appleseed's Birthday: Cook apple dishes and desserts, and have an apple-carving contest.

October 1 - National Pasta Month: Have a pasta feast.

2 - Phineas Fogg's Wager Day: Have a "casino night" party with a rented roulette wheel, card games, poker chips, and prizes.

9 - John Lennon's Birthday: Listen to the Beatles, and rent *A Hard Day's Night*, *Yellow Submarine*, or *Help!*

11 - National School Lunch Week: Have everyone

bring their own lunch in a lunch box.

12 - Columbus Day: Have an Italian feast at home, or "discover" a new Italian restaurant with your friends.

November 1 - National Author's Day: Celebrate a favorite historical author with period food and dress.

2 - Daniel Boone's Birthday: Take a nature hike.

3 - Sandwich Day: Have sandwich fixings for everyone to make their own "Dagwood" sandwich.

6 - John Philip Sousa's Birthday: Put on the marching music, or host a screening of *The Music Man*.

7 - Sadie Hawkin's Day: Have a Sadie Hawkin's dance where you invite only women—it's up to them to bring the men.

December 6 - Joyce Kilmer's Birthday: Have everyone write a poem to share.

10 - Thomas Gallaudet's Birthday: Communicate in silence for part of the party.

14 - Nostradamus's Birthday: Have everyone make silly or serious predictions for one another.

16 - The Boston Tea Party: Serve tea and cakes.

22 - Shorts Day: Have everyone wear crazy shorts.

Now you know that any day can be a "Best Party" occasion! Just for good measure, here are five more traditional holidays to celebrate:

VALENTINE'S DAY PARTY

A Valentine's Day party should be the embodiment of romance— from the invitations to the favors sent home with the guests at the end of the party. You might want to host a hearts-and-flowers brunch or have a simple and elegant dessert. The Wedding Shower and Anniversary Party chapters on pp. 11 and 67, respectively, might be helpful for additional ideas.

Invitations

Set the mood for a perfect Valentine's Day get-together by sending out heart-felt invitations:

- Make lacy heart invitations. Cut out heart shapes from red "velveteen" paper available at a hobby or crafts store. Glue the hearts onto white tagboard cut a little larger than the hearts. Glue lace trim on the excess tagboard to form a lacy outline around the heart. Write your party details on the back, and mail it to guests.

- Buy small heart-shaped boxes of candy, and write your party details on white tagboard. Cut the tagboard to fit inside the heart-shaped box, seal it up, and hand-deliver the invitation to your guests.

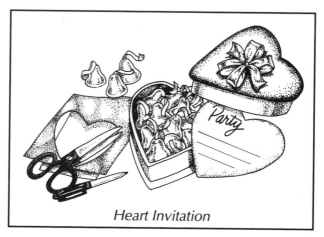

Heart Invitation

- Buy some little candy hearts that have love messages on them. Write your party details on red tagboard with white ink, and cut the tagboard into a heart shape. Place it in an envelope along with the little candies, or glue the hearts onto the invitation.

- Hand-deliver a red rose or carnation to each of your guests, with a small tag attached displaying your party details.

- Ask your guests to dress romantically in a red and white theme, or in the most romantic outfit they can find.
- Ask your guests to dress as a romantic hero or heroine.

Decorations
••••••••••••••••

Try some of these heart-stopping party decoration ideas:

- Adorn your party room with pink, white, and red crepe paper streamers. Or use a red-and-white theme, with accessories to match.
- Light lots of red, pink, and white votive candles, and set them around the room. Play romantic mood music.
- Decorate the center of the room with bunches of pink, white, and red balloons, or tie one heart-shaped Mylar balloon to the backs of two chairs, joining them together with ribbons.
- Make cookie bouquets by baking sugar cookies in heart shapes and pressing wire stems (like those used for flower arranging) into the backs of them. Decorate the hearts with red, white, and pink icing; gather them carefully together with ribbons; and set them at each place setting. Or place several cookie bouquets in a vase in the center of the table, all tied up with ribbons.
- Put photos of famous romantic couples at each place setting, and hang posters showing romantic movie scenes on the walls.
- Place roses at each guest's place setting, and set bouquets of flowers around the room.
- Cut out red and pink paper hearts, and hang them from the ceiling or tape them to the walls.
- Make large heart place mats from paper or felt, and create simple napkins from red fabric or fabric with a heart pattern.

Games and Activities
••••••••••••••••••••••••••••••

Here are some special games and activities, guaranteed to entertain the couples at your romantic bash:

- Make some love coupons for your guests—it's a fun and romantic addition to any Valentine's Day party. To do this, write up love coupons that are good for some activity or special treat that would appeal to couples. You might write down, "Good for one long kiss on demand." "Good for one dinner at a favorite restaurant." or "Good for time off from a least-favorite chore." Make at least three duds: "Good for taking out the garbage." "Good for one mandatory call to your mother-in-law." or "Good for hearing and correcting one major fault." Fold the coupons in half, mix them up, and place them in a heart-shaped box. Explain that each guest gets to pick a love coupon and that they are to oblige the request on demand from their partner at any time. Have them read their chosen coupons aloud to the group.

- Have each couple tell the story of how they met, where they went on their first date, or how they felt their "first time." You'll be surprised at how different their versions of the story are!

- Have all your guests reveal what they find attractive about their partner.

- Make up a romance by going around from guest to guest and having each of them add to the plot line. Ask the first guest to start the story with a lusty beginning. Stop after a few moments and go on to the next guest, asking him or her to embellish the story. Continue from guest to guest until all have added to the story and it's brought to a conclusion.

- Have each guest write down the worst opening line to a romance he or she can imagine. Then have all your guests read the lines aloud, one at a time—try not to giggle!

- Have everyone sit in a circle, and make each guest take a turn giving a popular phrase, song title, or quote with the word love in it, such as, "Love is blind." "How do I love thee . . . ?" or "Love Stinks." If someone can't come up with a phrase quickly enough, they're out. Play until you're down to the winner.

Refreshments

Eat and drink to your heart's content with these refreshment favorites:

Drinks

- Whip up strawberry daiquiris in the blender, and serve in tall cooler glasses. Mix together 1 1/2 ounces Daiquiri mix, 1–2 ounces light rum, 4 ice cubes, and five fresh or frozen strawberries, and blend till frothy. (You may omit the rum for tasty, non-alcoholic beverages.)
- Serve mimosas (champagne mixed with orange juice) with a strawberry at the bottom of each glass.

Luncheon Foods

- Quiche is an easy, make-ahead luncheon dish that will please nearly everyone (see pp. 146–47 for the recipe).
- Make a pink salmon mousse in a heart shape.
- Serve crab sandwiches on sliced French bread, with Cheddar cheese slices, bacon, and shredded lettuce.

Desserts

- Serve the cookie bouquets (see the Decorations section in this chapter) as dessert. Or make a giant chocolate chip cookie, and use it first as a centerpiece and then as a dessert.
- Serve croissants filled with fresh strawberries or cherry pie filling. Top with chocolate sauce and whipped cream.
- Cut small cantaloupes or honeydew melons in half, and remove the seeds. Cut out the melon flesh and put it aside, and then cut a small slice out of the bottom of each melon half so it will stand without wobbling. Fill the shells back up with cantaloupe or honeydew slices mixed with raspberries, blueberries, and strawberries. Or fill a large melon with a mixture of 1/4 cup yogurt, 1/4 cup honey, 1/4 cup coconut, and 16 ounces cottage cheese. Assemble sliced fruit around the melon for dipping.

• Fill crepes with pecan ice cream, and top with chocolate sauce.

Prizes, Gifts, and Favors

Here's what's fun to give and to receive at your Valentine's Day party:

• Box of candy.
• Bouquet of flowers.
• Romance magazine or novel.
• Theater tickets or movie passes.
• Bottle of champagne.
• Stationery, mug, or other item with "lips" on it.
• Poster of a hunk or a beauty.
• Romantic tape or CD.
• Romantic cologne.
• Massage oil.
• Mylar balloons with romantic sayings.
• Book of love poems.

ST. PATRICK'S DAY PARTY

St. Patrick's Day is a great time for a traditional Irish feast. Welcome the Irish and non-Irish alike to help you celebrate this "lucky" time of year.

Invitations

Try these invitation ideas, and your guests will be "wearing the green" in no time:

• Cut out green clovers from tagboard and green foil wrap. Glue the wrap onto tagboard, and add your party information with a green felt-tip pen. Mail in a green envelope.

- Buy a lottery ticket for each guest, and write your party details on a clover-shaped, green tagboard card. Attach the tickets to the cards with paper clips.
- Try to find small, inexpensive pins with a St. Patrick's Day theme (available at most gift, card, or stationery stores). Attach one to each invitation.
- Cut out a large potato from brown construction paper, and add a few eyes with a black felt-tip pen. Write your party details on the back.
- Buy a large bag of gold-foil-wrapped chocolate coins. Write your party details on the front and back of four or five coins, and mail them in a padded envelope.
- Buy a few lucky charms—a rabbit's foot, a medallion, a crystal, a lucky troll, and so on—and attach them to a card containing your party details. Mail them in a padded envelope.
- Ask your guests to wear as much green as possible.

Decorations

Your guests will be dancing a jig when you put them in the right St. Patrick's Day party mood:

- Cut out large shamrocks from green construction paper, and hang them on the walls.
- Cut out a large tree from brown and green tagboard, and attach it to one wall. Put your party food in crock pots, copper pots, and kitchen pots, and set the pots on a table near the tree. Buy a "rainbow" at a party goods supply or novelty store (or make one from construction paper or crepe paper streamers) and hang it on the wall, making sure one end lands near the tree, right at the food—the "pots of gold" at the end of the rainbow!
- Make a treasure chest from a box covered with gold gift wrap. Fill the box with gold-foil-wrapped chocolate coins, and leave it partly open.
- Decorate the room with lucky charms—horseshoes, rabbit's feet, medallions, "Blarney stones," four-leaf clovers, and good-

luck trolls.

- Accent with anything green—dyed daisies, green candles, bowls of green jelly beans, and green plants.
- Cut out large shamrocks from green construction paper or felt for place mats. Serve drinks in beer mugs, whether it's beer or not. (If it's beer, tint it with green food coloring.)
- Make an unusual centerpiece using potatoes: Cut out small paper shamrocks, tape them to toothpicks, and stick them into the potatoes. Surround the potatoes with gold-foil-wrapped chocolate coins.

St. Patrick's Day Centerpiece

- Set a large, smooth rock in the center of your table. Thickly color your lips with bright red lipstick, and make lipstick kisses all over the "Blarney stone."
- Get some posters of Ireland from a poster shop or some brochures about Ireland from a travel agency, and place them along the walls.

Games and Activities

Celebrate the fun-loving Irish with special St. Patrick's Day activities:

- Give your guests "instant" lottery tickets, and have them scratch the tickets or open their pull-tabs, one at a time.

- Hide lottery tickets or lucky charms throughout the house, and let your guests search for them. (But let them know they can have only one per person.)
- Have everyone write down as many superstitions as they can think of, such as, "Don't let a black cat cross your path." or "A broken mirror brings seven years bad luck." Read them aloud, and give a prize to the lucky winner who has the most on his or her list.
- One at a time, have your guests name something Irish. If someone can't name an item, they're out. Keep going until only one person is left, and award that guest a prize.
- Use an almanac to find some facts about Ireland. List them, along with some bogus ones. Read the list aloud, asking your guests to note which facts are true and which are false. Award a prize to the guest with the most correct answers.
- Read the following list of Irish-sounding names, and ask your guests which ones were born in Ireland: Roger Moore, Roddy McDowall, Rod McKuen, Patrick McGoohan, Ed McMahon, Edmund O'Brien, Carroll O'Connor, and Sean Connery. Have everyone guess until they can't guess any-more. Then reveal the answer, which is none! These people were born in London, London, Oakland, Queens, Detroit, Milwaukee, New York City, and Scotland, respectively.

Refreshments

Have your guests sample the tastes of Ireland at your St. Patrick's Day bash:

- Serve some traditional Irish dishes at your St. Patrick's Day dinner—corned beef and cabbage, new potatoes, Irish stew, or soda bread—and don't forget the beer!
- Offer your guests a do-it-yourself stuffed potato. Line up bowls of "tater" toppings—bits of bacon, diced ham, shredded cheese, cooked broccoli, cooked peas, sour cream, butter, and chives—and let your guests fill up their own hot baked potatoes.

- Serve potato skins. To do this, bake a bunch of potatoes, cut them in half, and scoop out the meat. Deep-fry the skins until crisp, and fill them with shredded Cheddar cheese, green onion, and crumbled bacon. Broil the skins in the oven until the cheese melts, and serve with ranch dressing.
- Make or buy large soft pretzels, and hang them around your guests' necks so they can munch on them while drinking beer.
- Wash everything down with green beer. There are a couple of green beers on the market, or you can tint your own keg with green food coloring.

Prizes, Gifts, and Favors

The topper to any St. Patrick's Day get-together is a special treat. Consider the following ideas:

- Lottery tickets.
- Lucky charms, such as a rabbit's foot, lucky troll, or horseshoe.
- Your secret recipe for stew or other Irish dishes.
- Six-pack of green beer.
- Sack of Irish potatoes or a bag of potato chips.
- Bag of gold-foil-wrapped chocolate coins.
- Stationery or other item with a rainbow design.
- Tape or CD of Irish folk songs.
- Poster of Ireland.
- Shamrock pins.

CINCO DE MAYO PARTY

Cinco de Mayo is a Mexican national holiday, recognizing the anniversary of the Battle of Puebla, when Mexican troops defeated Napolean's invading forces. The fifth of May is honored in Mexico with a Cinco de Mayo festival of dancing, music, and food. Hispanic Americans also celebrate it with special parties, parades, and cultural events. Host your own festival with Mexican costumes, food, and decor.

Invitations

Your Cinco de Mayo fiesta begins with an inspiring invitation:

- Invite your guests to your South of the Border party with travel brochures for Mexico—write your party details inside.
- Send your guests a small God's eye decoration (most craft books show how to make them from yarn and craft sticks), with your party information attached to it on a small card.
- Hand-deliver a small bag of tortilla chips with your party details written on the bag with a permanent ink, felt-tip pen.
- Give your guests a large, colorful paper flower, and tie your party information to the stem.
- Ask your guests to dress in a Mexican costume.

Decorations

Decorate your party room with color and imagination:

- Decorate with lots of colorful crepe paper, and hang a piñata

Piñata

from the ceiling. Piñatas are available at many craft, hobby, party goods supply, and discount stores. They're also fun to make with balloons, papier-mâché, newspaper strips, and paint. Fill any piñata with small presents, candies, pennies, and treats!

- Put Mexican rugs, flags, and sombreros on the wall, or hang a travel poster of Mexico to create a South of the Border atmosphere.

- Decorate your party room in the colors of the Mexican flag— red, white, and green—and use variations on the flag theme for place mats, wall hangings, and other accents.

- Play Spanish-language music, spirited guitar instrumentals, or mariachi tunes in the background to set the mood.

Games and Activities

Let the fiesta begin! Try some of these Cinco de Mayo party activities:

- Break the piñata. Have your guests blindfold themselves, hold a baseball bat or broomstick, and take turns trying to crack open a piñata (attached to your party room ceiling). When the piñata breaks open, treats will fall to the floor—have your guests scramble to collect the goodies.

- Play a popular game that everyone is familiar with (like charades), but throw them a curve—all your guests must use their little (or fluent) knowledge of Spanish as they play. (You might want to play a game where you can divide up into couples or teams so that guests can help each other out—or provide an English/Spanish dictionary.) If charades is played, for example, the English words are guessed, but the winner is the first team to provide the Spanish translation!

- Hire a Spanish-language singer to serenade your guests during mealtime.

- Give your guests a trivia quiz on some major historical events of Mexico, or name some famous Mexican heroes and have your guests guess who they are.

- Do the Mexican hat dance. (A library book on Mexican folk culture or a folk dance group can show you how it's done— then you teach your guests.)

Refreshments

Mexican food is a must at a Cinco de Mayo festival. You can have it catered or have each guest bring a dish. Here are some other refreshment ideas:

- Have everyone join in on the cooking of a big Mexican dinner. It's lots of fun when friends get together and prepare the meal.
- Serve Mexican beer, sopapillas, and nachos with salsa as appetizers while dinner is cooking.
- For dessert, make flan (a caramel custard) or serve ice cream rolled inside a light flour tortilla and drizzled with caramel and chocolate sauces.
- Find great "fiesta food" recipes in *Sizzling Southwestern Cookery* by Lisa Golden Schroeder (Meadowbrook Press, 1989).

Prizes, Gifts, and Favors

Consider the following Cinco de Mayo party gift possibilities:
- Jar of homemade salsa.
- Mexican cookbook.
- Bag of blue-corn tortilla chips.
- Copy of a movie set in Mexico, like *The Three Amigos*.
- Panoramic poster of Mexico.
- Large Mexican sombrero or serape.
- Colorful paper flowers.
- Reproduction of Aztec art or artifact.

FOURTH OF JULY PICNIC

The Independence Day picnic, celebrating the signing of the Declaration of Independence, is a tradition with most American families. Here are some tips for putting together a picnic, barbecue, luau, or potluck party at the pool, beach, or by the backyard sprinklers.

Invitations

Declare your Independence Day bash with one of these invitation ideas:

- Make "poppers" by writing your party details on small cards, stuffing them inside paper tubes, and wrapping them with crepe paper. Tie off the ends with ribbon, and fringe them with scissors. Mail in a cardboard tube, or hand-deliver.

"Popper" Invitation

- Cut out firecracker shapes from red tagboard. Glue glitter to the tips and colorful ribbon to the ends to make streamers, and write your party details on the cone of the firecracker. Place them in envelopes, and sprinkle extra glitter inside.

- Buy inexpensive American flags at a party goods supply store, and write your party details on them.

- If you're planning a luau (a great outdoor alternative to Fourth of July picnics), write your party information on postcards with pictures of the South Seas (or other body of water) and mail them to your guests. Or get some brochures on Hawaii at a travel agency, and write your party information in the margins. Or send guests a plastic lei (available at party goods supply stores), with your party details attached.

- Mail paper lunch bags with the party details written on them. Ask each guest to decorate the bag with a "patriotic" theme, and fill it with some favorite munchies to share at the party.

- Mail your invitations in large envelopes with gummed stars stuck all over them. Fill the envelope with star stickers or confetti so they tumble out when opened.

- Make your invitation on a piece of white paper cut out like a star, with "Spend the Night Under the Stars" written on the front. Enclose an R.S.V.P card that allows them to check either "Not in the stars" or "The stars are in your favor." Ask all your guests to wear only white.

- Ask guests to bring bathing suits and towels if you'll be near the water.

Decorations

Get the fireworks started with these holiday decoration tips:

- Set out small American flags stuck into hunks of white cheese or bowls of dip.

- Hang red, white, and blue crepe paper streamers from the ceiling. Decorate the patio or backyard with either white or red, white, and blue Christmas lights.

- For outdoor fun, serve food in beach pails or terra cotta flower pots. Fill a wheelbarrow with ice and cold drinks.

- Get out all your beach paraphernalia, and ask your guests to bring along anything they might have that would be appropriate at the beach, pool, or the great outdoors.

- Use red or blue bandannas for place mats or napkins, or buy inexpensive straw fans to use as place mats. Tie napkins to the handle of the fans for a decorative effect. Your guests can use the fans for cooling off when it's hot!

- Make an extra table for a big crowd by resting a large board on two sawhorses and covering it with a red, white, or blue tablecloth.

- Cover tables with red-checkered tablecloths, or buy inexpensive fabric in red, white, and blue and make your own tablecloths. Use two colors and two sizes of paper plates, one resting on top of the other at each place setting.
- Spread large beach towels or old sheets and blankets over the grass, sand, or dirt for picnicking.
- Hire a school or private band to play music.
- Play a John Philip Sousa marching tape for background music.
- Control bugs with bug lights or "zappers," and spray the yard with bug repellent an hour before the party. Citronella candles are a natural way to keep the bugs from your guests—light many of them for lots of protection and atmosphere.
- For a luau, float candles and gardenias or other flowers in the pool. Play Hawaiian music. Decorate your fence with torches, large fish nets, travel posters of Hawaii, or fake fish.

Games and Activities

Most Fourth of July get-togethers include the trek to a site where fireworks will be displayed just after sunset. But before the fireworks begin, try some of these party-pleasers:

- Give everyone—kids *and* adults—a squirt gun, and have a water fight.
- Get out the old favorites—volleyball, croquet, horseshoes, and lawn darts—and set them around the yard for your guests. Or have lawn games like sack races, three-legged races, wheelbarrow races, and tug of war.
- Any outdoor game or activity will be fun for both adults and kids—try baseball, kickball, soccer, kick the can, badminton, kite flying, and "picnic table" crafts.
- Divide your guests into groups, and have them act out some event from American history—make everyone guess what the event is. Or name several important dates in history, and quiz

the group on what happened on those particular dates.

- Make up box lunches, and have each guest bid for the lunch he or she wants.

- Have all your guests share what they like about living in America and what aspects they might change.

- Have each person talk about some unusual or out-of-the-way place in America he or she has visited.

- If you're having a luau, do the limbo, and give an award for the best Hawaiian costume.

- For a luau, have your guests make their own grass skirts from large paper bags, crepe paper, or other paper. Then have them all do their version of the hula to appropriate music. Take lots of photos with a Polaroid camera for mementos.

Refreshments

Here are some helpful suggestions for your next Fourth of July feast:

- A potluck is the easiest way to handle large crowds. See the Reunions chapter on p. 123 for ideas on how to organize a potluck picnic.

- If you're barbecuing, jazz up those plain old hamburgers and hot dogs! Grill the burgers and dogs to order, and let your guests choose from a large array of toppings to create their own bodacious burgers and humungous hot dogs. Offer guests these toppings: guacamole, pesto sauce, salsa, sour cream, chutney, melted hot pepper cheese, shredded Cheddar cheese, sautéed mushrooms, sautéed onions and garlic, green and red pepper slices, tomato slices, strips of bacon, pickles and relish, and your special "secret sauce"—catsup, mayonnaise, and mustard mixed together.

- Try a different way of serving burgers and beans. Place hamburger patties in large muffin tins, individual casserole dishes, or custard cups, and shape the meat to fit. Bake at 350° for 10 minutes. Turn the pans over, and dump out the meat onto paper towels to absorb the grease. Set them upright on plates, and top them with warm baked beans.

- If you're having a salad, here's an easy, eye-catching one that's guaranteed to please. (And for convenience, you make it a day ahead.) In a large glass salad bowl, layer shredded lettuce, 1 can sliced water chestnuts, $2\frac{1}{2}$ cups shredded, cooked chicken, 1 cup chopped celery, $\frac{1}{2}$ cup chopped green pepper, $\frac{1}{2}$ cup chopped red onion, $\frac{1}{2}$ cup mushrooms, and 1 package uncooked frozen peas. Spread 1 pint mayonnaise over the top of the salad to seal the layers. Cover and refrigerate for 8 hours. Before serving, add 6 ounces grated Cheddar cheese and 10 slices crumbled, cooked bacon.

- Scoop out one half of a watermelon (save or eat the watermelon). Fill the shell with raspberry sherbet, and smooth it down until it looks like "watermelon." Stick chocolate chips in two rows along each side to make the "seeds." Keep frozen until serving time.

- Dip fresh strawberries in melted white chocolate, and skewer them with toothpicks on a Styrofoam cone to make a "tree."

- Cut a pineapple in half, and cut the flesh into chunks. Mix the pineapple with maraschino cherries, and put the mixture in the pineapple "shell." Serve marshmallow sauce on the side, for dipping.

- Set a bottle of juice in an empty milk carton, and put a few flowers between the juice bottle and the carton. Fill the carton with water, and freeze. At picnic time, tear off the milk carton "mold" to reveal flowers set in ice all around the juice bottle. Serve the juice ice cold.

- It's not a summertime picnic or party without homemade ice cream. Try making fresh peach, fresh strawberry with mini chocolate chips, or vanilla with crushed candy bars.

Prizes, Gifts, and Favors

Have some of the following on hand to give away at your Fourth fête:

- Beach toy.

- Suntan lotion or oil.
- Sunglasses.
- Bandanna.
- Beach towel.
- Rattan beach mat.
- Visor.
- Squirt gun.
- Fourth of July or American flag pin, or anything with a flag motif!
- Gardenia corsages.
- Plastic or candy lei.
- Guidebook to Hawaii.
- Jar of macadamia nuts.
- Bag of Hawaiian potato chips.
- Hawaiian beer (Primo).

HALLOWEEN PARTY

The year's not complete without a come-as-you-aren't Halloween party. If you ever wanted to be Romeo in a school play or wondered how you'd look in a bunny suit, here's your chance. A Halloween party offers you and your friends an opportunity to return to childhood and live out your fantasies—at least for a few hours.

Invitations

Begin the haunting with a special invitation for your guests:

- Buy (or make from posterboard) the kind of masks that cover only the eyes and nose—they're usually found in discount and drug stores. Write your party details on the front or back in black felt-tip pen. Enhance them by cutting out "wings" and a beak nose from construction paper. Add colored feathers or other plumage, if you wish. Punch two small holes on either side of the mask, and tie thin ribbon streamers in them. Sprinkle glitter and sequins around the edges, using spray adhesive to make them stick.

- Hand-deliver small pumpkins with your party details written (in felt-tip pen) on the back, and a funny face drawn (or carved) on the front. Drop them off at a front door, ring the bell, and run!

- Cut out a pumpkin shape from orange tagboard, and use it as your invitation. Fill the envelopes with candy corns or pumpkin seeds.

- Mail a package of pumpkin seeds (available at most grocery stores) with your party details written on or glued to the back of the package.

- Design a newspaper ad or poster for a horror movie, with your party details woven into the ad—use the ads for the movie *Halloween* or some other scary show as your inspiration. Photocopy them, and mail to your guests.

- Ask your guests to come in costume. You can have a free-for-all where everyone chooses whatever he or she wants to wear, or have specific costume instructions such as:

  - Dress in styles specific to a certain era—'40s, '50s, '60s, or '70s.

  - Come as your favorite monster.

  - Dress in pairs (so that couples match each other in some way).

  - Come as your mentor, hero, or heroine.

  - Come as your favorite movie (as a character or as a unique aspect of the movie).

  - Dress as your favorite singer (have guests bring a tape, record, or CD, and hold a lip-sync contest).

  - Come as a famous cartoon character.

  - Come dressed as if you were eighty years old.

  - Dress as a child.

  - Come dressed as your partner's occupation.

  - Dress as your hobby.

Decorations

Haunt that house or party room with ghoulishly great decorations:

- Purchase small bags of "cobwebs," or make your own from fiberfill. Carefully pull them apart, and stick them to any rough wall or ceiling surface (or secure the ends with small pieces of tape). The webs look best when framing the front door or windows, but they can be stretched from a light fixture to a wall or table, too. Place several rubber spiders or other creepy crawlies in the webs, and hang the rest from the ceiling using black thread and tape.

- Buy several small orange and black votive candles and inexpensive holders to go with them, and place them all around your party room for a spooky effect. Add a few tapered candles, too.

- Pick up a few horror movie soundtracks—*The Rocky Horror Picture Show, Phantom of the Opera,* or whatever's available. If you have a VCR, rent some horror movies—*Night of the Living Dead, Halloween, Young Frankenstein,* or *Friday the 13th*—and play them in the background.

- Carve some pumpkins, turning them into hideous jack-o'-lanterns. Get creative, and make them as ugly as possible. You might even label them with the names of your guests and use them as place cards.

- Hang orange and black crepe paper streamers in every doorway so your guests have to brush them aside as they walk through.

- Have a "ghost" greet your guests as they enter your house or party room. To do this, blow up a large balloon, and tie it off with black string. Cut a tiny hole in the center of an old white sheet, and slip the string through. Let the sheet fall over the balloon, to form a "ghost." Draw two black circles for eyes, and hang the ghost (with the black string) from the ceiling by the doorway.

- Have a couple of scary characters greet your guests (and discourage unwanted spirits). To do this, stuff two sets of old clothes, one men's and one women's, to look like real bodies.

Place two chairs on either side of your doorway, and set the "bodies" on them. Find a couple of tall tables, short ladders, or boxes you can stack, and put them behind the chairs. Set two jack-o'-lanterns on top, just at the point where the heads should be, to make your bodies "come alive." For added fun, set one of the heads in one of the body's arms to make a "headless" host.

- Play scary Halloween sound effects records or tapes (available at record, drug, and discount stores).

- Have a mini-jack-o'-lantern centerpiece. To do this, cut the tops off oranges as you would a pumpkin. Scoop out the insides, and replace with a votive candle. Draw funny jack-o'-lantern faces on the oranges with a felt-tip pen. Lay a few gummy worms and rubber spiders around the table.

Games and Activities

Let the ghoulish games begin! Try some of the following Halloween party ideas:

- Gather the ghouls together for a costume-judging contest. You might want to award a prize just for best costume, or turn the contest into the main event, awarding prizes for ugliest costume, most embarrassing costume, most original costume, the costume that took the most work, the costume that took the most nerve to wear, and so on.

- You've heard of bobbing for apples? How about bobbing for olives in a martini! Fill enough plastic champagne or wide-mouthed beverage glasses for all your guests with 1 jigger vermouth and 3 jiggers gin or vodka. Drop 5 olives in each glass. Line the glasses around a table so that each guest has access to a glass. On the count of three, have your guests put their hands behind backs and bob into their martinis for all *five* olives at the same time, using only their tongues! Whoever collects all five first should raise his or her hand (it's impossible to yell, "I won!").

- Play "Pass the Pretzel." Gather a bunch of cotton swabs and curly pretzels, divide your guests into two teams, and line everyone up. Hand everyone a swab, and ask them to place one end in their mouths and put their hands behind their backs. On the count of three, stick a pretzel on the first player's swab, and have that player pass it on to the next player's swab. If it drops, the person who dropped it must pick it up and return it to his or her own swab. The first team that passes it to the last player wins.

"Pass the Pretzel"

- Play "Creepy Quotes." Distribute paper and pencil, and have your guests number their piece of paper from one to fifteen. Read aloud the following quotes from famous horror movies, and ask your guests to name the film it came from on their piece of paper. Award a point for each right answer—the guest with the most points wins.

  1. "It's alive!" (*Frankenstein*)

  2. "Even a man who is pure in heart and says his prayers at night may become a wolf when the wolfsbane blooms and the moon is full and bright." (*The Wolfman*)

  3. "Slowly I turned, step by step, inch by inch, and then I grabbed him . . . ." (*Abbott and Costello Meet Frankenstein*)

  4. "It's not Frankenstein; it's *Frankenstein* (Fränkenstēn). It's not *Igor* (ēgor); it's *Igore* (īgor)." (*Young Frankenstein*)

  5. "Three more days till Halloween." (*Halloween Party, II*)

6. "You'll just be staying the one night?" (*Psycho*)

7. "They're heeere . . . . " (*Poltergeist*)

8. "Heeere's Johnny!" (*The Shining*)

9. "Stay on the path. Keep away from the moors." (*An American Werewolf in London*)

10. "Is there someone inside you?" (*The Exorcist*)

11. "Make no mistake—this is not a human child." (*The Omen*)

12. "Wake up! They get you when you sleep. They grow out of those pods." (*Invasion of the Body Snatchers*)

13. "What have you done to its eyes?" (*Rosemary's Baby*)

14. "Michael! Did you hear your father? Out of the water—now!" (*Jaws*)

15. "You wouldn't be able to do these awful things to me if I weren't in this chair." "Oh, but you are, Blanche. You are!" (*Whatever Happened to Baby Jane?*)

- Have a lip-sync contest if your guests are dressed in '40s, '50s, '60s, or '70s costumes. Play songs from those years, and have each person do a number.

- Hold a pumpkin-carving contest. Give each guest or couple a pumpkin, and ask them to carve it creatively. Award prizes for the best, worst, ugliest, and most creative pumpkins.

- Have each guest act out a horrible scene from a horror movie. You might write some titles on slips of paper to get people started, such as *Psycho, Halloween, Jaws, Nightmare on Elm Street, Frankenstein,* and *The Bride.* This is fun, easy, and perfect for Halloween.

Refreshments

There's nothing like a Bloody Mary at a Halloween party! And here are some other fright night treats to try:

- Welcome your guests with a mug of "witches brew." Combine in a large pan 1 pint cranberry juice cocktail, 1 bottle Burgundy wine, 2 sticks cinnamon, 1 lemon (thinly sliced), 1 cup water, ½ cup sugar, and 6 whole cloves. Cover, and heat on low for 1 or 2 hours. Carve out a pumpkin, rinse thoroughly, and pat it dry. Draw a hideous face on the outside of the pumpkin with a black felt-tip pen. Serve the brew in the cleaned-out pumpkin shell.

- "Frozen pumpkins" make a perfect dessert for hungry guests. You'll need 1 orange per guest, vanilla ice cream, and canned pumpkin pie mix. (For this recipe, 1/2 gallon of vanilla ice cream mixed with an 8-ounce can of pumpkin pie mix will fill eight to twelve oranges. Adjust the amount of ingredients for your number of guests.) Cut the tops off the oranges as you would a pumpkin, scoop out the insides (save the pulp and juice for breakfast), and pat them dry. Draw little jack-o'-lantern faces on them with a black felt-tip pen. Soften the ice cream, and then scoop it into a bowl and stir in a can of pumpkin pie mix. Blend thoroughly. Scoop the mixture into individual oranges and freeze. Set the "pumpkins" out five minutes before serving.

Prizes, Gifts, and Favors
• •

Consider these trick-or-treat tidbits for your Halloween gang:

- Pair of passes to a horror movie.
- Pumpkin (carved or uncarved).
- Mask.
- Horror movie soundtrack.
- Trick or treat bag filled with gourmet candy.
- Gummy rats and worms.
- Paperback mystery novel.
- Tape of an old radio show, such as *The Shadow, Mystery Theater,* or *War of the Worlds.*

Chapter 15

Private screening parties are becoming increasingly popular as more people purchase state-of-the-art televisions, more quality programs are offered on networks and cable, and more videos become available to the public for home rental.

TV Guide and a little imagination will help you get a number of television-based party ideas. You might want to host an election-night celebration, a mini-series premiere, a beauty pageant gathering, a PBS auction night, a "Saturday Night Live" bash, or a late-night talk-show party. If you and your friends are sports fans, you might enjoy a Super Bowl party, an Olympic event, a World Series gathering, or a televised tennis match party.

You might simply want to rent a newly-released movie, an old favorite, a musical, or a horror film, and design your party theme around the particular selection. If you need specific ideas for TV parties, here are four different themes for private screenings you might want to host for your friends:

ACADEMY AWARDS AND EMMY AWARDS PARTY

Have an Academy Awards or Emmy Awards night, and invite your friends to come dressed in formal gowns and black tie (just as they dress for the real event), complete with sunglasses. Or have everyone dress as one of the characters in a film or TV show nominated for an Oscar or Emmy. Serve a sit-down dinner or just have cocktails and hors d'oeuvres, with a fancy-dessert finale.

Invitations

Choose just the right invitation idea to announce your glittering evening:

- Cut out Oscar shapes from tagboard, and cover them with gold gift wrap. Write your party details on the back.

- If your party will be black tie, cut out a bow tie from black tagboard and write your party information in white ink (or vice versa).

- For an Emmy party, cut out and make TV sets from tagboard. Write your party details on the screen.

- Cut out pictures of the Oscar or Emmy nominees from magazines and photocopy them. Write question marks around them, or put speech bubbles over their heads with some funny comments in them. Add your party details around the edges of the invitations.

- Cut out stars from silver paper to use as invitations. Fill the envelopes with gummed stars or confetti.

- Send ballot forms along with each invitation so your guests can fill them out before the party begins. Ask them to bring the ballots to the party.

- Cut out oversized theater tickets from tagboard, and write your party details on them—try to make them resemble real tickets. Mail a pair to each of your guests.

Theater Ticket Invitation

Decorations

Star in your own "Best Party," and create a gala event with these decorating tips:

- Buy posters of movie or TV stars at a poster shop, and hang them on the walls near your TV screen. Give them away as prizes if you plan to have games at your party.
- Cut out star shapes from white tagboard, and put glitter on them. Hang them from the ceiling in your party room.
- Make a large, colorful chart of the Oscar or Emmy nominees, with photos from the tabloids or *People* magazine, and score the nominees during the evening.
- Hang a few famous movie or TV titles and quotes on the wall, such as "Frankly, my dear, I don't give a damn." "I'm getting frisky, Marion." or "Father Knows Best."

- Find items relating to the nominations for best picture or best TV series, and set them up as a centerpiece for your table.

- Make voting ballots for the awards, and use them as place mats at your table. Set out some trophies, and label each "Oscar" or "Emmy." Cover the table with star-studded fabric.

- Play the soundtrack from one of the nominated movies or taped portions of nominated TV series until the awards ceremony begins.

- Decorate your party room with black and silver streamers draped from the ceiling to the walls. The streamers provide a formal-looking and impressive atmosphere for some serious celebrity-viewing.

Games and Activities

Heighten the anticipation and excitement of the awards night with these party-pleasers:

- Have everyone place bets on who will win in each category. Once the nominations are announced and published, make up a sheet with all the categories and nominees so your guests can circle their guesses before the awards show begins. Award a prize to the guest with the most right answers.

- Provide rubber-tipped dart guns for your guests so they can shoot the unpopular winners on the TV screen.

- Visit the library and research past Oscar award winners—there are several books available, but one very good one is *Fifty Golden Years of Oscar: The Official History of the Academy of Motion Picture Arts & Sciences* by Robert Osborne (ESE California, 1979). Write down the titles of some movies and their best actor and best actress winners. Scramble them up on a sheet of paper, and ask your guests to match the movies with their stars and to name the year the movie came out. You can do the same match-up game with TV stars and their series for the Emmy Awards.

- If you have the Silver Screen edition of "Trivial Pursuit," play an informal game during the commercials by reading off the questions and having your guests shout out the answers. Award a prize to the "star" player.

- Write down a few famous lines from award-winning movies or TV series, and have your guests guess what movie or show you're quoting from.
- Give each guest or couple a part from a movie or TV show to act out, and have everyone try to guess the movie or show.

Refreshments
••••••••••••••••••••

And the winner is . . . lots of food and drink! Try the following:

- No private screening party is complete without popcorn. Flavor each batch of popcorn with spices and seasonings (see the Birthday Party chapter on p. 62 for flavored popcorn ideas) and serve it in real popcorn bags (available at party goods supply stores).
- Offer a variety of foreign beers to honor foreign films and celebrities.
- Choose a food theme from one of the more popular nominated films or series, such as western food for *Dances with Wolves* or bar food and/or Boston recipes for "Cheers."
- Make it a lazy night for all, and have a bunch of pizzas with lots of toppings delivered to your home.
- Provide typical theater snacks, such as Jujubes, Jordan Almonds, Dots, Junior Mints, Raisinettes, and Milk Duds.
- Serve an array of TV dinners on TV trays for your Emmy party.
- Have ice cream bonbons or Dove bars for dessert.
- For a black-tie event, serve champagne and fancy hors d'oeuvres and desserts.

Prizes, Gifts, and Favors
••••••••••••••••••••••••••••••••••••••

Be the host with the most—try these gift give-aways at your private screening get-together:

- Movie or theater tickets.
- Poster of a famous celebrity.
- Movie or celebrity magazines.
- Inexpensive movies or videos.
- Tabloids, such as the *Enquirer* or the *Star.*
- Box of microwave popcorn.
- Box of theater candy, such as Jujubes or Sugar Babies.
- Book of movie or TV trivia.

GRAMMY AWARDS AND COUNTRY MUSIC AWARDS PARTY

Throw a dinner dance for your Grammy or Country Music Awards party (or for the alternative American Music Awards or MTV Video Music Awards). Ask your guests to come dressed as rock stars, or in country-style overalls, boots, bandannas, and cowboy hats.

Invitations

Prepare your guests for a night of music and fun with a special invitation:

- Cut out record shapes or musical notes from black tagboard, and write your party details on one side. Mail these invitations in large envelopes.

- Buy some photo postcards of your favorite recording artists at a record store, and write your party details on the back. Just add a stamp and mail.

- Buy the sheet music to some of the nominated songs, and write your party information along the lines. Photocopy and send them to your music-loving guests. Or use blank sheet music as a background for your invitations. You could even make some of the letters look like musical notes.

- Cut out musical notes from black construction paper, and write your party details on them in white ink.

- Send ballot forms along with each invitation so your guests can fill them out before the party begins. Ask them to bring the ballots to the party.

Decorations

Your party room will be alive, with the sound of music (and some dandy decorations):

- Hang posters of your favorite recording artists and the evening's nominees on the walls of your party room.

- Cut out musical notes from black tagboard to hang from the ceiling.

- Make a wall chart for recording the winners.

- Rent a mirrored ball and some strobe lights to add extra sparkle to your "dance floor."

- Play tapes or CDs in the background before and after the "main event."

- Set out blank sheet music for place mats.

- Keep the color scheme black and white, with red accents.

- Hang some titles and lines from songs around the room, such as "I Wanna Hold Your Hand," "Stand by Your Man," or "Like a Virgin."

- Set your table with new-wave props, such as colorful jewelry, bright scarves, and record-album jackets.

- If you're celebrating the Country Music Awards, use red checkered tablecloths and napkins, and set up a country-looking centerpiece using brown eggs, hay, a gingham chicken, and a few bandannas.

Games and Activities

You'll be a winner if you add some of the following to your evening of popular music and awards excitement:

- Have everyone bet on the award winners. Give a prize to the guest who makes the most correct predictions.

- Provide rubber-tipped dart guns for your guests so they can shoot the unpopular winners on the TV screen.

- During the commercials, play an informal game of "Trivial Pursuit," using the "Entertainment" questions. Read off the questions, and have your guests shout out the answers. Award a prize to the guest who gets the most correct answers.

- Write down lines from songs on a sheet of paper, and ask your guests to write down the song titles and recording artists.

- Have a dance contest or a square dance.

- Play an informal game of "Name That Tune." Before the party begins, record just a few seconds of each of your records, allowing about ten seconds of silence between songs. Distribute paper and pencil to your guests, and then play the tape for them, asking everyone to "name that tune." Replay the tape and name the songs, allowing your guests to check their answers. Award a prize to the guest with the most correct answers.

Refreshments

Try the following award-winning assortment of musical munchies:

- Have a pot of cheese or chocolate fondue for guests to dip into as they get hungry. Serve bread and vegetables with the cheese; serve fruit, marshmallows, nuts, and snack food with the chocolate.

- Offer your guests an all-you-can-eat salad bar. Set out bowls of salad fixings and bottles of dressing, and tell everyone to help themselves. You might even ask your guests to bring along a bowl of their own favorite fixings.

- Ask a bakery to make a cake in the shape of a musical note or a record album.
- Make a pan of brownies, and slice it into large squares. Top with vanilla ice cream, banana slices, strawberry slices, fudge sauce, whipped cream, and a cherry—quick, easy, stunning, and delicious!

Prizes, Gifts, and Favors

The following make great musical mementos:

- Tape or CD by a nominated artist.
- Blank tapes.
- T-shirt, featuring a popular rock star or one of the nominees.
- Concert tickets.
- Poster of a popular singer or group.

SUPER BOWL AND WORLD SERIES PARTY

The Super Bowl and the World Series are great occasions for a party. Use some of the New Year's Day party ideas, such as having your guests come dressed up as sports figures or in a favorite team's colors. Sporting events are perfect excuses for an office, neighborhood, or just-for-friends gathering.

Invitations

Set the stage for non-stop sports fun with these invitation ideas:

- Cut out footballs or baseballs from construction paper, fold them, and write your party details inside.
- Buy some football or baseball cards at a sports or variety

store, and write your party details on the back.

- Photocopy an old football or baseball program or ticket, and write your party details on it.
- Photocopy part of the sports page, substituting your party details in one of the columns.

Decorations

Add to the gridiron or diamond excitement with these decorating suggestions:

- Hang posters of the team or star players.
- Cut out footballs or baseballs from tagboard, and hang them from the ceiling.
- Decorate your party room with your favorite team's colors.
- Write up a few statistical questions (you can get them from a sports almanac or a friend who's a sports buff), and hang them on the walls.
- Rent or devise a small set of bleachers to sit on. Or arrange your furniture in a half circle to simulate a stadium.
- Use a Ping-Pong table as your serving table, and decorate it with white tape yard lines and drinking straw goalposts to look like the gridiron.

Gridiron Serving Table

- Mark out your party room with yard lines, and set up a few homemade goalposts. Or re-create the ball park with baselines, bases, and a home plate. Have guests sit along the first and third baselines, and put the TV set at the pitcher's mound!

- Use old football or baseball programs as place mats.

- Make a centerpiece of footballs (or baseballs), helmets (or caps), pennants, and peanuts. Or add a touch of whimsy with some Ace bandages, Ben-Gay, crushed beer cans, and Gatorade.

Games and Activities

Games and activities are great ways to keep the action going before and after the game, and during commercials:

- Have everyone place bets on the winners, or have a football or baseball pool. Your guests can win money (for a real pool) or sports-related prizes.

- Provide rubber-tipped dart guns for your guests so they can shoot at the opposing team on the TV screen.

- Play the Sports edition of "Trivial Pursuit," or ask questions from the "Sports" category of the Genus edition.

- Use a sports almanac to find information about various baseball or football players. Write down some questions, and hang them on the walls. Ask your guests to write down their answers between innings or quarters. Award prizes to the winners.

- Take a break, and go play some ball.

- Place penny bets on everything that comes up, from who will win the coin toss to which beer commercial will be on next.

Refreshments

Hungry armchair quarterbacks and bench-warming sluggers will love any of these noshing notables:

- Set out a cheese and bread hors d'oeuvre that fans can tear apart as they watch the game: Buy a large round loaf of

French bread and cut halfway into it in a crisscross pattern. Insert slices of Cheddar cheese in one direction and Monterey Jack cheese in the other direction. Top it with margarine, Parmesan cheese, garlic salt or powder, and black pepper; then broil until the cheese is melted.

- Have chili and corn bread—it's a great crowd-pleaser since it's simple, filling, and delicious.
- Have peanuts or pistachios in the shell, trail mix, or bread sticks with cheese dip—they're just right for snacking.
- Provide Kielbasa hot dogs, burgers, soft pretzels, and other stadium mainstays.
- Hire some neighborhood kids to dress as vendors (or do it yourself), and serve the food from boxes tied around their necks.

Prizes, Gifts, and Favors

Score a touchdown or a home run with these party give-away ideas:

- Tickets to an upcoming game—professional, amateur, college, or high school.
- Home-team pennants.
- Sweatshirt or T-shirt with the home-team logo.
- Sports almanac or fact book.
- Baseball or football cards.

HOME VIDEO PARTY

Rent a newly-released movie or an old classic, and invite a few friends over for a home video party. The newly-released movies are always a hit, even if they bombed at the box office, but don't forget favorite movie musicals like *Bye Bye Birdie* or *West Side Story*; or classics like *The Godfather, Citizen Kane,* or *Gone with the Wind.* You might want to have a horror film party and show *Frankenstein* or *Nightmare on Elm Street.* Just design your party around the movie's theme, and you'll be sure to have a memorable night.

Invitations

Plan your great movie escape well, and let everyone in on the fun with a special invitation:

- Draw some symbol from the movie, such as a shower curtain if you're planning to show *Psycho* or a gorilla for *King Kong*, and use it for the front of your invitation. Write your party details on the back.

- Some poster shops have postcards of old movie scenes or celebrities that you can use for your party invitations. Write your party details on the opposite side, apply a stamp, and mail.

- Look through a tabloid or movie magazine, cut out a picture of the star of the movie you're showing, and glue it to a card. Write your party details on the back.

- Buy a few tabloids or movie magazines, and cut out pictures of celebrities. Put speech balloons over their heads, and write your party details inside them.

- Buy popcorn bags from a party goods supply store or theater, and write your party details right on the bag. Fill the invitation envelopes with a few popcorn kernels.

- Make some oversized theater tickets from tagboard, and write the title of the movie and your party details on them.

Decorations

"Best Party" movie screenings always feature imaginative, exciting decorations. Try some of the following:

- Buy some movie posters, and hang them in the party room.

- Hang items from your ceiling that relate to the movie, such as little spaceships for *Star Wars* or stuffed gorillas for *King Kong*.

- Make a centerpiece from a collection of items related to the movie, such as a lemon, garter belt, lipstick, wig stand, and old trumpet for *Some Like It Hot.*

- Make place mats from pictures of movie stars by pasting them to construction paper and covering them with clear Contact paper.

- Arrange your party room to resemble the movie's set. For example, if you're showing a scary movie, use a few old Halloween masks for a centerpiece, dim the lights, and put candles around the room.

- Write down some quotes from the movie, such as "Play it again, Sam." or "Beam me up, Scotty!" and display them around the room.

- Greet your guests in a costume appropriate to the movie.

- Make an eye-catching centerpiece with a huge bowl of popcorn set on some old movie reels. Make place mats from popcorn bags.

- Set up your wet bar or a table to look like a theater candy counter.

Games and Activities

Try these ideas to keep everyone entertained at your private screening party:

- Have an intermission since there won't be any commercials during your video screening. That way guests can stretch their legs and get more drinks and snacks.

- Take a few notes as you watch the film, and give your guests a quiz at the end of the movie.

- Play movie-title charades.

- Take turns quoting from different movies, and have everyone guess the movie title.

- Do a little research on the stars of the movie, and write up a few trivia questions.

Refreshments

Hungry movie buffs will flock to these "flick" food items:

- Have popcorn and candy snacks for the "moviegoers."
- Make a vegetable dip from 2 mashed avocados and $\frac{1}{2}$ sour cream. Serve with carrot and celery sticks, zucchini and green pepper slices, and cherry tomatoes.
- Provide a selection of toppings for a make-your-own sundaes intermission.
- Have homemade Chinese food or get take-out, and put it in colorful cartons (available at party goods supply stores and card shops), with chopsticks.
- Serve refreshments appropriate to the movie, such as mint juleps for *Gone with the Wind*, bananas for *King Kong*, or spaghetti for *The Godfather*.

Prizes, Gifts, and Favors

Movie magic will linger on with these special mementos:

- Coupon good for a free movie rental.
- Videotape of a classic movie.
- Movie tickets.
- Huge bag of pre-popped popcorn.
- Blank videotapes, for taping TV movie favorites.
- Memorabilia from the film, such as a picture of Rhett and Scarlett for a showing of *Gone with the Wind*.

MORE EXCUSES FOR A PARTY

Chapter 16

You are now set up to host a "Best Party" for almost any occasion. But remember, a "Best Party" needs your enthusiasm and special flair. You can turn *any* idea into a winning party theme. Here are some more imaginative ideas to help you get started:

Charades Party

Have some friends over for an evening of charades. The game can be based on a particular theme—horror movies, TV shows, or children's books, for example—and you can either play the official way, breaking sentences into words and syllables, or have your guests act out scenes. There are also several good versions of charades available in boxed game sets.

Treasure Hunt

Buy or make a creative treasure box full of fun items, and tell your guests they're going "hunting." Write creative clues on pieces of paper, and place them around the house, the neighborhood, or the city. Assign couples or teams, and send them out on foot or by car. Make the clues cryptic so they're not too easy to follow, and send your guests on wild goose chases when they make a wrong guess!

Roaring Twenties

Ask your guests to come in costume, and have your party room set up with different gambling games—roulette, cards, and dice. Play music from the twenties, and let everyone dance.

International Evening

Ask your guests to come dressed in costumes of their heritage or ancestors, or as a famous foreigner. Have everyone bring dishes representative of a particular region as well as some interesting historical facts, regional games, or other items to share with the group.

Toga Party

Have everyone dress in Roman togas. Send out invitations on small parchment scrolls, serve Greek or Italian food, drink wine from goblets, and play "Drop the Grape into Caesar's Mouth." To do this, divide your guests into couples, and have one member of the pair lie on the floor while the other tries to drop grapes into his or her mouth from a standing position. The pair who "catches" the most, wins.

Murder Mystery Party

Buy a murder-mystery-party book or game (available at book, party goods supply, game, and department stores), and have your friends solve a mystery. Or host a large party with some friends playing the role of suspects, and have the rest of the crowd be the sleuths. Ask the extras to come dressed as their favorite detectives (or villains).

Clambake

Have a clambake at the beach or in your backyard. Corn on the cob and steamed, fresh sausages make delicious side dishes to any seafood bake or boil. Serve shrimp cocktail, have a crab feed, or feast on abalone.

Gone with the Wind Garden Party

Turn your backyard or party room into a Southern garden with flowers, ribbons and bows, parasols, and other gracious-living touches. Ask your guests to dress as Southern belles and gentlemen (formal sundresses and formal wear are fine). Hire a few neighborhood teenagers to serve the food. Rent tents and umbrellas, and play croquet. Hang pictures of Scarlett O'Hara and Rhett Butler wherever you can, play a *Gone with the Wind* trivia game, and end with a special screening of the movie.

Texas Barbecue

Ask everyone to dress as cowpokes or cowgals, in jeans, checked shirts, twirly skirts, boots, and string ties. Barbecue ribs on the grill, have a hoedown and square dance with a real caller (or use a record), and arrange for a hayride in the country.

Soup Group

Get your friends together on a regular basis, and try out a new soup at each meeting. Serve salad and bread with the soup, and plan an activity, such as charades, cards, games, or storytelling.

Fashion-Victim Party

Did you ever regret keeping an item of clothing but couldn't throw it away because it was (a) so expensive, (b) a gift from someone special, (c) something you *had* to have, or (d) such a bargain? Well, you're not alone—share your "regret" by hosting a "fashion-victim" party. Ask your friends to come dressed in a "fashion-don't," and spend the evening laughing and sharing stories about fashion "mistakes." End the party with a garment trade or auction.

Taste of America Party

Have each guest or group of guests set up a table with different city themes. For example, if the city of choice is San

Francisco, set the table with a toy cable car, flowers, and sourdough bread. Each table should feature a different part of the meal—appetizers, salads, soups, the main course, desserts, or drinks. The San Francisco table could feature buttered sourdough bread for the appetizer, crab cocktails for the salad, artichoke bisque for the soup, sukiyaki for the main course, orange mousse for dessert, and wine from a California vineyard for the drinks. Have each group dress in typical attire from the area.

Ski Party

You don't have to have snow to have a ski party. Just have your guests dress in snow bunny or ski bum apparel, start up a nice fire, stick a few resort names on the walls, add some fake snow, and complete the scene with a centerpiece made from goggles, ski wax, and a pair of broken skis. Serve stew or chili, and hot drinks. Talk about skiing!

Mother and Daughter Tea

No matter how old your daughter is, she's just the right age for a mother and daughter tea. Have several mothers and daughters over for a luncheon or tea, and ask your daughter to help with the preparation. Make it a dress-up party, or have moms dress like daughters and vice versa. Stage a make-your-own sundae event, and have all your guests take turns answering some stimulating questions such as, "What's most important in our friendship?" "What do you like best about your mother (daughter)?" or "What will we be doing in five (ten, and so on) years?" With some imagination and a bit of re-tooling, you can also come up with a father/son party.

Lottery Party

Have everyone bring a certain number of lottery tickets. Scratch the tickets together (slowly—for suspense!). Award any winners with a wrapped prize—a book about how to stop gambling, ten more lottery tickets, or a book about contests.

Mortgage Payoff Party

A mortgage payoff is a big event in everyone's life, and a perfect time to celebrate. Bring the lucky guest(s) of honor joke gifts such as brochures for a cruise, ads for new homes, bank-account promos, or a highbrow magazine like *Town and Country*.

Income Tax Party

April 15th is the day to hold your income tax party. Set the table with old newspapers and plain paper plates, and mail your invitations on IRS forms (available at public libraries). Ask your guests to wear rags!

Tacky Party

Have all your guests dress in their tackiest clothes and accessories—taped glasses, plaid pants and print shirts, bell-bottoms, and outdated shoes. Ask them to bring tacky gifts to exchange with other guests. Serve tacky food—American cheese sandwiches on white bread, chocolate milk, and Fig Newtons for dessert. Play tacky games—Musical Chairs, Bingo, Go Fish, Spin the Bottle, and Simon Says.

Invite-a-Friend Party

At your next gathering have each guest invite a friend (someone new to your group). It's a great way to meet new people.

Favorite TV Show Party

Have your guests come dressed as characters from a popular television show on the night the show airs, such as "Star Trek: The Next Generation," "Northern Exposure," or "Roseanne." Hang pictures of the stars from the program around the room, and decorate the room to look like the set of the show. Serve appropriate food, and play a trivia game based on the program.

Car Road Rally

Drive around town with a map, and put up paper plates with trivia questions on them along the route for drivers to read and answer. Type up directions for the course, and make sure your paper-plate pit stops have questions about certain points of interest along the route. You can make your map simple and direct or cryptic and full of clues and riddles to challenge your guests' knowledge and memory. Have guests follow the map directions and watch for paper plate markers as they drive around town. (For safety, have a "navigator" accompany each driver, and instruct everyone to pull over to read the signs.) Meet back at a favorite restaurant to see who got lost, who got all the answers, who had the best time, who had the fewest errors, and so on. Award a trophy to the pair with the most correct answers.

Sporting Party

Gather the gang for a sports party—volleyball, softball, roller-skating or -blading, biking, bowling, touch football, or swimming—whatever the season and equipment permit. There's no need to decorate much since the party will be held outside or at a sports facility, but try to keep the food appropriate to the sport. And get creative! For a bowling party, have your guests dress in funny bowling shirts (they can get them from a thrift shop), and then go to a hamburger joint or ice cream parlor after all the pins are down. Or, for a biking party, set up a course similar to the road rally with checkpoints or questions along the way. Make the final destination an informal restaurant, and return home on the same route to collect all the paper plates.

Now that you have the basics, a check list, some creative suggestions, and a number of themes to work with, you're ready to throw a "Best Party" special event. Good luck on your next get-together!

The Best Baby Shower Book

by Courtney Cooke

Finally, a complete guide for planning baby showers that's chock-full of helpful hints, recipes, decorating ideas, and activities that are fun without being juvenile.

Order # 1239

The Best Wedding Shower Book

by Courtney Cooke

The complete guide for planning wedding showers. Contains time- and money-saving ideas for decorating, food, innovative gifts, and fun, creative games.

Order # 6059

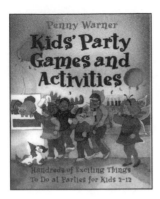

Kids' Party Games and Activities
by Penny Warner

This is the most complete guide to kids' party games and activities on the market. It offers illustrated instructions and trouble-shooting tips for hundreds of activities—with ideas ranging from easy to elaborate, and traditional to contemporary. Perfect for parents of kids ages 2 through 12.

Order # 6095

Kids' Holiday Fun
by Penny Warner

Every single month of the year, families can turn to this comprehensive guide for yummy holiday recipes, decoration suggestions, instructions for fun holiday activities and games, party ideas, and crafts. This is the ultimate holiday activity book covering 35 holidays, including New Year's, Valentine's Day, St. Patrick's Day, Fourth of July, Halloween, and Christmas.

Order # 6000

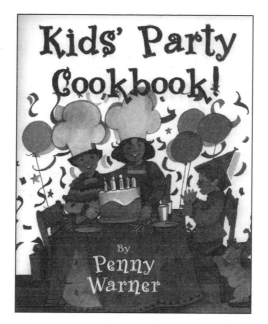

Kids' Party Cookbook

by Penny Warner

Warner has fun ideas for every meal, including mini-meals, such as Peanut Butter Burger Dogs and Twinkle Sandwiches; creative snacks, such as Aquarium Jell-O and Prehistoric Bugs; creative desserts, such as Spaghetti Ice Cream and Doll-in-the-Cake; holiday fare, such as Candy Cane Parfaits for Christmas and Jack O'Lantern Custard for Halloween. (Ages 8 and up)

Order # 2435

Also from Meadowbrook Press

♦ *The Best Baby Shower Book*
The number one baby shower planner has been updated for the new millennium. This contemporary guide for planning baby showers is full of helpful hints, recipes, decorating ideas, and activities that are fun without being juvenile.

♦ *The Best Wedding Shower Book*
Valuable time-tested advice on how to plan and host the perfect wedding shower with great games, activities, decorations, gift ideas, and recipes.

♦ *Games People Play*
With 180 word, drawing, memory, and trivia games for adults, adaptable to a variety of party themes, this book is funnier, faster-paced, and more entertaining and challenging than any other book of party games.

♦ *Instant Parties*
If you have tableware, music, a wee bit of know-how in the kitchen, and a few this-and-thats to use as props, this book will show you how to whip up any one of fifty instant parties in a matter of hours without even breaking a sweat.

♦ *Memorable Milestone Birthdays*
Here's the only book on how to host memorable milestone birthday parties. Included are creative ideas for themes, invitations, décor, entertainment, and refreshments.

♦ *The Mocktail Bar Guide*
Here is a must-have addition to your collection of bartending and party-planning books. This one-of-a-kind guide offers 200 delicious, alcohol-free drink recipes for nondrinkers, designated drivers, expectant mothers, and anyone who enjoys great-tasting drinks. Royalties from the sale of this book support Mothers Against Drunk Driving (MADD).

We offer many more titles written to delight, inform, and entertain.
To order books with a credit card or browse our full
selection of titles, visit our web site at:

www.meadowbrookpress.com

or call toll-free to place an order, request a free catalog, or ask a question:

1-800-338-2232

Meadowbrook Press • 5451 Smetana Drive • Minnetonka, MN • 55343